W9-BWH-423

WITHDRAWN

Praise for Joanne Palmisano's

Salvage Secrets
and
Salvage Secrets Design & Decor

"It is an ideal book for anyone considering salvage in design. . . . Often books on design are either practical and plain or only full of photographs with little guidance on how to create the same look in one's own home. *Salvage Secrets* . . . manages to be a design book with both."

—*Portland Book Review*

"Joanne demonstrates throughout her book the ease with which recycling and reuse can be incorporated with function and style. Architects, designers, and do-it-yourselfers should all have a copy of this book in their home design library."

—*New England Home*

"[A]n invaluable first step in the salvage-for-design journey."

—*Fine Homebuilding*

"A highly inspiring design book with everything you need to know about integrating recycled, reclaimed, and salvaged materials in to your home . . . Joanne Palmisano offers innovative strategies to transform your interior design ideas in both big and small ways with a little salvage creativity."

—Karin Lidbeck-Brent, national magazine stylist

"Emerging from today's design landscape that can appear contrived, pristine, and disposable, *Salvage Secrets Design & Decor* is a refreshing demonstration of how reclaimed materials can translate into an elevated yet deeply personal design statement. Palmisano's approachable, practical writing combined with Teare's engaging photography make this book a must-read for anyone serious about sustainable and personal design."

—Aaron Danzig, Williams-Sonoma, Inc.

"If you're new to actually using salvaged items, like I am, that's where reclaimed material evangelist, designer, and blogger Joanne Palmisano comes in. Her new book, *Salvage Secrets*, is the ultimate guide to getting started. When you finish the book, you'll be armed and ready to search for your own trash-into-treasure find."

—HGTV, *Design Happens*

STYLING
with
SALVAGE

3 1526 05149318 4

STYLING *with* SALVAGE

Designing and Decorating with Reclaimed Materials

JOANNE PALMISANO

photography by SUSAN TEARE

THE COUNTRYMAN PRESS

A division of W. W. Norton & Company

Independent Publishers Since 1923

Copyright © 2018 by Joanne Palmisano

Photography by Susan Teare unless noted in the Credits

All rights reserved
Printed in China

For information about permission to reproduce selections from this book, write to
Permissions, The Countryman Press, 500 Fifth Avenue, New York, NY 10110

For information about special discounts for bulk purchases, please contact
W. W. Norton Special Sales at specialsales@wwnorton.com or 800-233-4830

Manufacturing through Asia Pacific Offset
Book design by LeAnna Weller Smith
Production manager: Devon Zahn

The Countryman Press
www.countrymanpress.com

A division of W. W. Norton & Company, Inc.
500 Fifth Avenue, New York, NY 10110
www.wwnorton.com

978-1-58157-462-3

10 9 8 7 6 5 4 3 2 1

To Gabrielle,
the Next Generation to
Make a Difference

conte

Introduction

Welcome to the Salvage Club

Hello, my name is Joanne and I have a problem. I'm totally addicted to old stuff, vintage goods, salvaging, junk—whatever you want to call it, I can't get enough. Mixing old and new when styling homes has been my passion since, well, forever. As a kid, I loved searching for old bottles in the backyard to display on my dresser. I'd spend hours in my parent's "junk room" trying to create something out of old wood, metal, and scraps of fabric. (Thankfully, none of my childhood masterpieces survived.) Today, as an award-winning interior designer, stylist, DIY/craft specialist, DIY Network-contributing designer, and author of two internationally acclaimed books, *Salvage Secrets* and *Salvage Secrets Design & Decor* (both W. W. Norton), I'm thrilled that I get to do what I love every day. In the ever-growing vintage-inspired design industry, I'm honored to meet, share, and talk with other like-minded souls about our undying passion for all things old, used, and collectable.

Anyone who's passionate about pieces with a past knows it's hard to explain their unique appeal. Sometimes, it's the hunt, or the find, or maybe the thrill of getting a good deal that compels me, but in every case it's the stories behind these objects that keep me looking for the next cool thing. Styling with salvage is not just about the love of vintage, or the way it makes your home look, it's also about reusing materials, understanding where they come from, and making a difference to our environment. If you can't pass a secondhand shop without wondering what unique knickknack might be in there for the taking, or if you're constantly finding new crafts to make out of stuff in your basement, or if you hear a crazy out-of-this-world story about an old door and know that you just have to have it in your home, then welcome to the club. You're just like me!

This book shows you how to blend, mix and match (or not) old things with new stuff, and it also explains why it's so important to incorporate these materials into your home, especially in today's world.

My goal is to fire up your passion for collections, inspire your creative repurposing ideas, and amaze you with stories of folks who have made their home unique by using vintage and repurposed goods. An increased demand for these materials leads to increased recycling, which is one of the best ways we can help our environment, save our natural resources, and improve our economy. That's a triple win!

Equally important, this fast-growing industry creates and supports thousands of jobs, from trade professionals to flea market vendors to antique store owners to salvage shop partners to large companies (and their employees), right down to the individual artisans and tradespeople who craft with old stuff. In reusing salvaged items and bringing jobs back to our local economy, you really can make a difference.

I'm thrilled and excited to once again feature exceptional photography by the amazingly talented Susan Teare. Alongside her team, Lindsay Raymondjack and Susan Black-Turner, Susan makes my work, and the work of others, shine in her photographs. I could not have done this book without her. We were once again honored to travel around and visit some incredible people who have incorporated reclaimed materials into their homes. I appreciate everyone who invited me into their spaces and let me style their rooms, and who shared their passion for vintage and salvage.

I hope this book inspires you to create your own home style that speaks to you and about you, and that using reclaimed materials will truly help you change the way you live and view the world.

xoxo Joanne

Emily and Calvin Sellers's Umland Street Sunday Haus, a rental cottage on their Carmine, Texas, property, is filled with romance and character. Talk about extreme recycling: The previous owners moved the entire cottage there from a farm in New Ulm, Texas. Emily and Calvin added a new tin roof and porches, and continuing the previous owners' passion for bringing old and new together, they filled it with unique finds. With its iron beds, vintage mirrors, antique textiles, and reclaimed-wood walls, this place is bursting with meaningful pieces that speak to Emily and Calvin's joy and love for all things with a story and a past.

Before You Start, A Few Reminders

How to Have Fun with Finding Your Style

I've met so many amazing people who love to do what I do—work, live, and design with old materials. You, too, will find yourself meeting new friends, joining fellow salvagers at fairs, and sending texts to celebrate finds with other folks who get it. Have a great time and know that you are part of a community. The single most important thing is to have fun. Don't get overwhelmed by all the fabulous styles out there, just focus on what speaks to you. Working with older materials is like assembling a jigsaw puzzle; sometimes you don't know what the picture will look like until you put all the pieces together. At times, this requires a willingness to handle the unknown, but if you learn about your material, how it works structurally, and see all the ways other people use it, then you can go in armed with the knowledge that your design will be a winner. And what's more fun than completing a stylish puzzle?

Understanding the Challenges

Working with salvaged material can be a challenge, but that can be half the fun too. There are many builders, architects, and designers who love working with these materials because of the creative thinking it requires. Seek them out through your local architectural salvage shops, antique shops, and recycled centers. If you love doing it yourself, then chat first with the folks at the places where you get your stuff—you will no doubt find them to be exceptionally knowledgeable about the materials and pieces.

Don't Be Nervous

Not sure where to begin? Just start small. Collect poker chips, old school desk chairs, vintage books with blue covers, or even something as simple as mason jars. Once you have these collections started, then work on how

Simple pieces of scrap wood, left in their natural state, line the walls of Tricia Rose's home in San Rafael, California. With eclectic flair, Tricia has a clever way of decorating, including placing old railroad spikes in the wall to hold up an old workman's lantern. Vintage wooden pulleys and a boat cleat make for unique decorative accents. A piece of lamb's wool is thrown over a secondhand swivel chair to add warmth. Welcoming and comfortable, this is a perfect corner for relaxing and reading, created in a budget-friendly way.

to style them: in a display on a wall, on a table, or on your mantel. Even these small projects can get pretty addictive!

It Can (Almost) Always Be Done

One of the most common things I hear is that when homeowners ask their builder or contractor to use reclaimed material, they respond by saying it can't be done. Well, I'm happy to report that most of the time it can be. Perhaps the contractor has never done it that way, and so they are reluctant to try. But by showing them pictures, such as the ones you see in this book, applying some gentle persuasion, and maybe engaging in some mild bribery (hello, homemade chocolate chip cookies), it *can* get done. But before you go all hog wild with ideas, you should first have a pretty good understanding of what your project will cost. Often the materials may cost less than they would new, but labor costs can

This cottage on Tybee Island, Georgia, showcases designer Jane Coslick's work with color and vintage finds. This old oak claw-foot table was painted in layers of green, red, and cream, which are reflected in the colors of the chairs. The cozy dining space in the kitchen of her office cottage shows how mixing and matching styles and eras can work if you use colors to pull it all together.

My Design Manifesto

HERE'S MY ELEVATOR PITCH: It's important to have an appreciation for quality materials and furnishings that are built to last. It's imperative not to be wasteful. And it's all about finding and keeping things that have meaning to us. You'll find lots of new pieces in my design work and in my own home, but I do try hard to thoughtfully incorporate vintage, repurposed, recycled, and reclaimed elements as much as I can. When I head out to find materials and products for my designs, I try to think about these four concepts:

1. **Anti-waste:** Is the company thoughtful about waste? Do they work hard to reuse what they can and manage all their own waste by-products? Do they have recycled products available?

2. **Built to Last:** Are the things I'm purchasing built to last? Is the furniture dovetailed; is the wood solid? Is it from a sustainable forest? Will I be throwing this away in two to five years or will it stand the test of time?

3. **Sustainability:** There are many types of sustainability, and we could discuss this term forever. What I consider is this: Are the social groups who produce the product treated fairly? Was the environment harmed in creating it? Do the economics of the product make sense? Basically, it's important to pay a fair price for a good product made by people who are rewarded for their work.

4. **Trends Versus Classics:** Every day there is a new "trend" online. If we tried to keep up with them, we would be changing out our furniture and decor weekly. Think about your home as a canvas and the walls and flooring and fixtures as the backdrop. I like to work with classics on these surfaces, and then if I want to get trendy, I usually do so in the soft goods—pillows, bedding, and decor.

bump up the price of the project. So be prepared to really crunch the numbers before moving forward.

Get Your Hands Dirty

If you want a reclaimed-wood wall, then get out there and search the piles at the salvage shop. Spend some time cleaning and sealing and getting them ready to install. The same is true for furniture pieces. Take an old dresser and clean it up and paint it. No matter the project, there is nothing like the satisfaction of doing the work yourself. This is especially true when you create something pretty to look at when the work is done (and you've saved money along the way).

Understand That Things Take Work to Get Them Ready

We all love to walk into a salvage yard, vintage fair, or antique shop and pick something up for a dime. But this isn't a realistic expectation. The fact is, many people had already worked to get an item ready for your consideration. They had deconstructed a building, wrestled pieces onto the back of a truck, drove them back to a workshop, and fixed, cleaned, and displayed the items, be it in a brick-and-mortar store or a booth at a fair. Pay a fair price. Research the value of the materials and have a good understanding of your budget for the items you want. Understanding the value of these items only makes getting a bargain all the sweeter!

1

Defining Reclaimed

What Does It All Mean?

Reclaimed material goes by a million names. Okay, maybe not a million, but you get my point. Don't worry. Honestly, almost all of them are interchangeable and none are wrong. In my first two books, *Salvage Secrets* and *Salvage Secrets Design & Decor,* I used the word *salvage* to describe all the items that were given a second chance at life, whether it was a piece of furniture or a piece of glass. For me, materials that are saved from destruction are things that are reused, reclaimed, repurposed, restored, recycled, salvaged, antique, or vintage. It's all good, in my opinion. The world of secondhand items and materials can get a bit confusing when dozens of seemingly interchangeable words are used to describe it all. As a designer who specializes in using these materials, I've tried to put some structure and meaning behind each of these terms.

As a textile expert and owner of The Textile Trunk, a company that sells vintage and antique textiles online and at vintage fairs, Wendy Lewis likes to surround herself with antique materials and furnishings she finds throughout the world. Her passion for their history shines through in every room in her Vermont home, filling her house with romance, color, and texture, as exemplified by this antique dresser and 18th-century French fabric panel.

Reuse

One of the easiest ways to be environmentally friendly is to reuse your own things. No additional energy is used to create a new product or involve the recycling process. Just by arranging your materials in a different way, you can change the look of your rooms. I love to get people to think outside the box when redoing their own homes. Can you paint your dining chairs in a bold color? Use stain or paint on your cabinets instead of buying new ones? Move that dresser into the bathroom? Place all your prints on one wall instead of having a single one on many walls? These styling tips are just a few examples of how you can reuse your own materials first.

Reclaim

The word *reclaim* is one of the most common terms used to describe secondhand stuff. Reclaiming almost always refers to wood: antique wood, vintage wood, heritage lumber, and secondhand dimensional lumber. When looking for old wood online, I usually search with the word *reclaimed*, because it's in so many of the names of the companies that salvage it. Throughout this book, you'll see examples of various woods and a variety of ways to use them: in tables, counters, wall hangings, and much more.

Repurpose

One of the fastest-growing trends in the design industry is repurposing. Whether it's metal baskets used as light fixtures, dressers turned into bathroom vanities, or doors made into headboards, the trend is everywhere. The word *repurpose* generally refers to using an item for something that is totally different than its original purpose. Repurposing is one of the most creative ways you can change up old stuff. When you look at an old piece, see if there is a different way you can incorporate it into your home.

Jennifer and Fred Myers have spent years building the guest cottage on their property, Jennifer's Gardens, in Austin, Texas. They often host concerts, weddings, and special events there, and they wanted the design of the property to reflect their passions. This cozy bedroom is just one example of how you can use architectural salvage pieces to create exceptional focal points in a room. With a reclaimed wood mantel and vintage mirror, both from Johnson City, Texas, and some handcrafted encaustic Mexican cement tiles, they created a fireplace feeling without the fire. These three items put together make a big impact in a small space.

The showroom at Salvage Works, in Portland, Oregon, is a great place to learn about reclaimed wood materials. The artwork here is by Benjamin Alexander Clark, one of the employees. The chair was reupholstered by Revive Upholstery & Design, also in Portland. This is an example of the great connections within the reclaimed community. Rachel and Preston Browning, the brother and sister owners of Salvage Works, take pride in sharing the stories of where the materials come from. The cool side table on wheels is made from four reclaimed hand-hewn beams that are from an Oregon barn built in 1904. Here, they are displayed in a fun loftlike atmosphere, but I can also see three of them lined up in front of a long couch in a contemporary home or modern farmhouse. Browsing shops like these can provide you with a great education on different materials, as well as insight on ways you can use them in your own design.

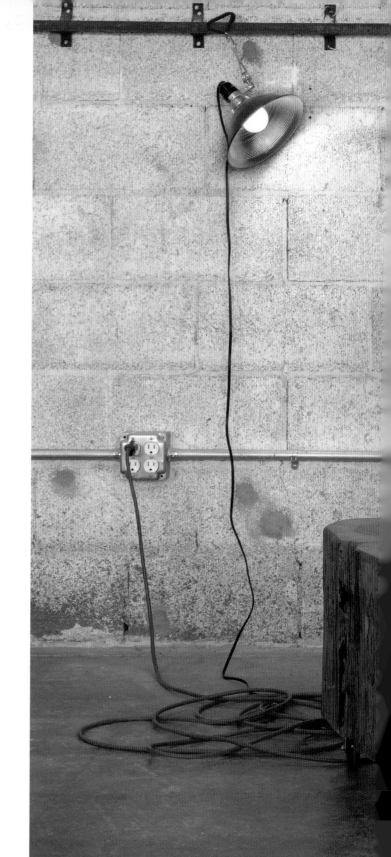

Birds of a feather stick together! Seriously in need of a craft fix one night, I went down to the basement and found an old baseball. I had a bag of feathers left over from another craft, and I'm never without a glue gun. So with some scissors and hot glue I started attaching the feathers to the baseball to make this unusual ornament. To re-create this, start on one side, forming a bottom. Then work your way up so that the tips of the feathers come out the top. Smaller feathers can get tucked into spots that need a little love. It doesn't take much to transform secondhand items sitting around your own home. This craft brought me back to the days of being in my parents' junk room, pulling things together. This time, however, the result is a keeper.

My twin sister, Rosanne, and I made this vanity by repurposing an old midcentury dresser we found at The Salvation Army. We made sure to get a piece with the right-sized width for the sinks and faucet. Using the paper template that came in the box with the sink, we drilled out the holes in the vanity for the faucets, and used a jigsaw for the sink hole. We then sanded it down and painted it a glossy white, spraying the handles silver. We let a plumber do the rest. If we can do it, you can too!

Where to Get What—at a Glance

BOOKS: Library sales and discounted secondhand bookstores.

COSTUME JEWELRY: Garage, church, and rummage sales.

FURNITURE TO CUT OR PAINT: Household goods recycling center.

GLASS VASES: Goodwill, The Salvation Army, Habitat for Humanity, or similar stores.

LIGHTING: High-end antique pieces: Conant Metal & Light, Rejuvenation, and other similar shops. DIY project: a rebuild center or Habitat for Humanity.

OLD OFFICE CHAIRS: Used office-supply stores and college warehouse sales. (I like to make side tables out of the metal bases of these chairs.)

OLD ROPE: Local shipyards, boat mechanics, and yacht clubs.

OLD SWEATERS: Goodwill, The Salvation Army, and rummage sales in the fall.

PORCH POSTS: Architectural salvage shops. (Use posts to make farmhouse tables.)

QUALITY ANTIQUES: Local antique stores or big antique fairs such as Brimfield, in Massachusetts, or Round Top, in Texas.

RECLAIMED WOOD BED FRAMES AND FURNITURE: Stores such as West Elm, Pottery Barn, Sundance, Vermont Farm Table, or custom made (ask at your local architectural salvage shop).

RECYCLED GLASS/PORCELAIN TILE: Tile shops like Fireclay, Bedrock Industries, and other artisan shops.

RECYCLED METAL HARDWARE: Online for cabinet knobs, drawer pulls, sinks, and lighting. For a piece of metal to cover an old coffee table, try a local metalwork shop.

SHIPPING CONTAINERS: A local shipping company or metal scrap yard, and ask around.

TEXTILES: Online at www.textiletrunk.com, local secondhand shops, or church shops.

TUBS AND SINKS: Local architectural salvage shops or rebuild centers.

VINTAGE BOOTS: Online at sites like Poshmark, Tradesy, Etsy, and eBay.

VINTAGE BOWLS, PLATES, AND SILVERWARE: Antique fairs and local vintage shops.

VINTAGE MIRRORS: Local furniture consignment shops and antique spots.

Lace tablecloths can be transformed into shower curtains, sweaters can be turned into pillows, old wood paneling can become a vintage-inspired sign, or an old desk can evolve into a bathroom vanity. As a contributing designer for DIY Network and other DIY magazines and sites, I spend a lot of time making something out of something else. And after a while, repurposing just becomes "second" nature.

Restore

When you find an old piece, an antique, or a collector's item, it might just need a good cleaning if you're lucky. But sometimes your purchases require a little restoration work.

Joints might need to be reglued or tightened. Claw feet of an old tub may need some repair, or a chip fixed. A lighting fixture might need to be rewired. But other than some restoration work, these pieces stand on their history and original purpose. Bringing something back to life is an easy way to add character to your home. If you alter an old piece of importance that you acquire, most likely that piece will lose a fair amount of its monetary value. So really do your homework. When in doubt, before you make any drastic changes, email a picture of your new find to an antique appraiser. For a small fee the appraiser will give you an assessment.

Recycle

This one is a biggie, because it could be considered interchangeable with any of the other keywords noted here. But in design, I like to use the term *recycle* when referencing tile, countertops, lighting, sinks, carpeting, furniture, and more items that have been made with "typical recycled/recyclable material" such as glass, textiles, metal, and paper. I'm happy to say that the demand for recycled-content materials and products is on the rise—helping keep these materials out of our already overflowing landfills and saving energy and virgin ore. Both the design world and homeowners are searching for materials that look and feel new but that have been made with recycled content.

Salvage

Salvage is all about rescuing stuff. That's why you see a lot of architectural shops using that word, because they rescue materials from old buildings, homes, barns, and warehouses and save them for us to use. A big thank you to all the folks who do this—it's a lot of hard manual labor and we appreciate it!

Antique

This term usually refers to valuable pieces of furniture or fixtures that

Glass

GLASS CAN BE RECYCLED AGAIN AND AGAIN AND NOT LOSE ITS QUALITY. It can be recycled in a powder form that, when mixed with concrete, makes an aggregate that looks like stone for a countertop. It can be formed into the size of small pebbles or cullet (small pieces of furnace-ready recycled glass). Recycled glass can also be turned into kitchen ware, glassware, countertops, shelving, tile, and much more. The possibilities for recycled glass seem endless. Unfortunately, a fair amount of glass is still heading to our landfills, and so the more we demand recycled glass products, the more it will be recycled.

are about 100 years old and older. Antiques are things that you don't want to cut up and repurpose because of their value and importance in our homes and history. There are many ways to learn more about pieces you already own or are looking to buy. Antique appraisers, the antique shop owners themselves, and online sites are all great resources. Researching is half the fun!

Vintage

This is the buzzword of the day and can describe things that are a mere 20 years old or a century old. *Vintage* is often used instead of *antique* because it's trendier, though the line between the two can be blurred. So whether you're looking for a midcentury sideboard, a 1980s rock band T-shirt, or a 1970s dresser, you can use the word *vintage* to help your search.

DIY

AT LEAST ONCE A WEEK SOMEONE ASKS ME WHAT DIY STANDS FOR. It stands for Do-It-Yourself. Through the thousands of DIY tutorials online, on TV, and on YouTube, you can figure out how to make anything yourself—within reason, of course. DIY isn't all about building or repairs, it can also refer to homespun and homemade crafting. I'm thrilled to see the resurgence of interest in making things. People are realizing how appealing it is to gather together with friends and strangers to create something. I love how relaxing it is to do crafts, and I will take any opportunity I get to do a DIY project. Some people have a weakness for midnight snacks . . . I have midnight crafts. Some days I'll experiment with paper bags and markers, or twigs and scrap yarn I picked up at the secondhand shop. Other days, I'm full-on manipulating metal and wood beams. It totally depends on the project and the mood I'm in. I hope you get inspired by the DIY projects and the interesting designs homeowners have showcased in this book.

2

The Fun and Importance
of Salvage

The Difference You Make By Celebrating Our Past

In my role as a designer, I encourage my clients to take pride in their ability to express style through vintage and repurposed material. I help them better understand the materials that go into their homes. Not only can they decide what materials to use, but they can choose where those materials come from. With approximately one-third of today's waste coming from the building industry, these choices are no small matter.

As you know, it's commonplace today to see vintage and salvage materials used in interiors. These uses can be small, like reusing glass jars in decor, or they can be larger scale, such as incorporating salvaged bricks into the

Revive Upholstery & Design, in Portland, Oregon, reupholstered this chair using Pendleton wool fabric. The owner, Leland Duck, and one of his employees took a day and a half to complete the project. It's important to understand the amount of time and energy that goes into quality upholstery. Creating an heirloom piece that will stand the test of time takes real craftsmanship. Here, they stripped off the old finish and let the natural grain shine through by using only a nontoxic paste wax. This stunningly crafted piece seamlessly blends a modern fabric with old wood.

architecture of the home itself. From recycled metal cans to vintage life buoys to furniture reused with a splash of paint, age-old and reclaimed materials come in many shapes and sizes. Items salvaged from your attic or someone's home, factory, or barn can add character to your space. Whether you repurpose an item or use it for its original purpose, you're saving pieces that were built to last and that are harder to find in today's disposable society. Not a single person I know has not been excited or touched by a salvage, vintage, or family heirloom story that they heard after admiring a piece in someone's home. This is important to understand, because what we put into our homes truly does speak to us and about us in so many ways.

Reusing—A Great Place to Start

To change the look of your own spaces, the first step is to see what you have that you can style differently. As a stylist, I get to go into people's homes, move things around, and get their rooms ready for a photographer to take a picture. Homeowners are shocked to see how I put their own pieces together, and they often ask me to leave the items as I placed them. Sometimes, you just need a fresh eye.

What Makes Older Trees Different?

UNLIKE NEW TREES THAT ARE FARMED, OLDER TREES HAVE MORE GROWTH RINGS AND ARE DENSER, GIVING THEM A UNIQUE GRAIN. Sometimes reclaimed wood from old buildings is the only way to have certain wood species in your home (the American chestnut, for example, has all but disappeared due to blight in the early 1900s). Comparing new woods with their older reclaimed ancestors is amazing; the older wood has a richness and character that newer wood can't touch. But the look of the salvaged wood is just one part of its appeal. Where the wood came from and the story behind it adds another element to your design and home.

My client, Gideon Pollack, gave me very few guidelines when renovating an outdated townhouse his family uses as a second home and vacation rental property. Just "work your magic and do it within a reasonable budget"—that was my brief. So with simple design ideas and a few bold statements, this Stowe, Vermont, townhouse was transformed from generic to gorgeous. To go from bland to stunning, the little bar area needed only a small piece of granite, which was left over from the countertop project (an alternative was to pick up small remnant pieces at a local granite and marble stone yard for a small fee), and some recycled tile at Fireclay Tile, from their Debris Series. The cow painting was picked up at Stowe Kitchen Bath & Linens. With a little paint and some small recycled pieces, you can give most any space a whole new look.

By gathering all the pictures from around the house, removing most of the frames, and hanging the art, this guest bedroom now has the cozy, welcoming feeling of a bohemian cottage. The 1970s owl lamp that had been languishing in the basement for years has been transformed with a coat of white paint, the addition of an old shade with its torn fabric removed, and some fun faux crystals on wire. Secondhand white bedspreads, vintage wool blankets, and a handcrafted rose rug add character and individuality to the room, and show off the workmanship and artistry of the past.

after

before

These old balusters waiting to be discovered at Restoration Resources, in Boston, are just some examples of the thousands of salvage materials available today. Because these balusters are too short to meet today's building codes for stairs, they can't be used for that purpose again. But think of the dozens of ways you can reuse these amazing architectural pieces: Single-pane windows can be turned into gorgeous indoor mirrors, and doors too small for today's doorway openings make perfect pantry doors, or even linen closet doors. In repurposing one piece at a time, we change the way we build, decorate, and live.

after

Basin Harbor, in Vermont, is undertaking a renovation of each of its rooms, guest spaces, and public areas with my help. These lodge rooms needed a little love. Instead of getting rid of everything, I reused the bed, side tables, dresser, and chair, knowing that by changing their surroundings they would look totally different. With new bedding, fun table lamps, some paint and wallpaper, a crisp wainscoting wall, and a new rug, this room is transformed. On the opposite walls are old frames found in the attics on the property. They were left in their natural state or were painted in an antique brass color.

before

Many years ago, Kim and Cliff Deetjen, interior designer and architect, respectively, purchased their heirloom mahogany server from an antiques dealer at the Brimfield Antique Show, in Massachusetts, for their Vermont home. Sitting proudly on top is the Tiffany & Company antique sterling silver Paul Revere Reproduction tea set that had belonged to Cliff's grandmother. Add in the gorgeous design of the blue-pigmented plaster walls with a wax finish, and you can't help but feel the elegance of this room.

Left: In 1886, the Seward and Webb family purchased land in Vermont to create an extensive model architectural farm and estate, which today is called Shelburne Farms, a National Historic Landmark. This custom-made door handle still resides on an early 1900s horse barn, which is filled with detailed custom cabinetry and woodworking rarely seen in modern construction. In 1972, the family made the property a nonprofit organization that still leads the way in innovative, sustainable practices in farming, education, and farm-to-table produce. This handle is one small example of exceptional craftsmanship.

Right: These vintage lockers that Carol and Randy Dupree found at ReUser Building Products, in Gainesville, Florida, helped create a walk-in closet in their master bathroom. This vintage find does double duty by creating privacy and adding storage space, and is a great example of how a single piece can be used as the aesthetic highlight of a room, as well as being a structural and functional part of it.

Recycling—Reducing Our Consumption of Energy and Raw Materials

The fact is that many "new" products on the market are made from recycled content. For example, when folks say they love a "new" carpet I used in a design project, I thank them and let them know that 80 percent of the carpet was made from recycled content. This often causes a bit of confusion, because that carpet is new. The point is, brand-new gorgeous materials, lighting, fixtures, furnishings, carpeting, tile, and even bedding can be made from recycled goods. Using these products is a great way to enjoy designing with the new stuff, while feeling good about reusing old stuff. Sometimes there's a 90–95 percent savings in making a product out of recycled materials, such as aluminum cans. Finding out a little bit more about recycled materials, their reuse options, and the energy saved is just as fun as using the item itself. When a recycling program is efficient, it helps reduce the use of raw materials, lowers energy emissions, and creates jobs. Metals, glass, and plastics are the most commonly recycled materials. It takes a lot less energy to melt recycled glass than it does to create new glass from raw materials. So when planning a refurbishment, why not support one of the hundreds of companies that have incredible home design products made with recycled materials?

Giving History a Chance to Speak Again

My mother tells me stories of her childhood in rural Vermont, about moving into the woods in the summer with her parents and working the land and cutting select trees by hand. They camped, washed dishes in a stream, and cooked over an open fire. My mother remembers these times fondly. I also think about my husband's grandfather, who made his daughter's entire bedroom set, including the bed, side tables, dresser, trunk, and armoire with marquetry (inlaid work made from small pieces of various woods) made from old cigar boxes.

At the Country Living Fair in Atlanta, my friends, Cari Cucksey, antique and salvage expert and host of the HGTV show, *Cash & Cari*, her husband, Vincent, mother, Edna, and father, Mark, all work together at their booth, with baby Orion sleeping in the Airstream. The wider family, including aunts, uncles, and cousins are all involved in the business too. Whether it is promoting her paint line, RePurpose, and their shop in Holly, Michigan, or selling antiques at a few shows and presentations a year, they do it as a family. Her passion for repurposing came from her grandparents, who lived through the Depression and gleaned great joy in bringing things back to life and usefulness. Cari's love for the items she finds is apparent in her work, home, and presentations. That she gets to do all of this with her family is priceless.

It's still her bedroom set today. I can only imagine how much time, creativity, love, and thought went into those pieces. We can respect and admire the craftsmanship and energy of times past by using these materials and pieces in our designs today. When I look at older pieces of furniture, reclaimed old-growth wood, custom-made trim and molding, or even elegant 19th-century tapestries, I always wonder what people's lives were like when those pieces were hand-chiseled, cut, or sewn. I'm always flabbergasted at the low price of many antique pieces.

I've had these old jars since my husband and I bought a house at auction. We discovered dozens and dozens of them in the dirt-floor basement. The tiny house was not livable when we bought it, but with some serious sweat equity, and the help of a two-man construction crew, we made it our home. These old jars are a regular reminder of how hard we worked to create a space to start our lives together. Now, in our new home (which was once an old camp on the lake that we deconstructed, recycled, and rebuilt—using tons of salvaged material), I use these jars as candleholders and flower vases. Looking at them as I sit outside and enjoy the sunset over the water, I appreciate all that I have and the great work I get to do.

Carol and Randy Dupree spent five years turning this 125-year-old Bainbridge, Georgia, warehouse into a unique home, learning the tales of the warehouse along the way. The couple is delighted to share stories of their materials with their guests, who are amazed and thrilled to learn more about the home. The kitchen is fun and inviting. Wood from old bowling alley lanes (found on Craigslist) was turned into countertops, and the island base was made up of secondhand Formica toolboxes from a hospital. The upper cabinets were made from old sash windows. Pulling all these reclaimed pieces together, plus the warehouse's open floor plan, makes for a space that is more "fun bar" than private kitchen.

THE FUN *and* IMPORTANCE *of* SALVAGE // 45

So many of them are affordable, and I think to myself: If that were hand built today, the asking price could be in the thousands or hundreds of thousands of dollars! But antiques are not about getting a deal. They're about respecting our past and appreciating our present and future.

Celebrating Craftsmanship, Tradespeople, and Our Past

Our society has become more disposable, and it's often easier (and cheaper) to replace something than it is to repair it. In past centuries, however, things were built to last, and our parents, and their parents' parents, repaired and rebuilt things. They celebrated craftsmanship and took pride in their possessions. I'm thrilled to see a resurgence in our appreciation of quality handcrafted materials from our past. Your home is a place to express your style, personality, and your experiences through what you choose to bring into it. Bring joy into your home. If an old basket from your childhood days makes you happy, bring it in to your design. Let the soul of that item seep into your heart and bring you happiness.

What to Look For in Old Upholstered Furniture

LELAND DUCK, AN UPHOLSTERER BASED IN PORTLAND, OREGON, REMINDS US THAT PADDING CAN BE REPLACED. With this in mind, look for a solid frame made from real hardwoods or, in the case of bar stools, sturdy metal. The older the piece, the better the quality. Many exotic woods are not available on the market today, and younger pieces tend to be made from particleboard or plywood rather than hardwood.

Leland Duck founded his company, Revive Upholstery & Design, in 2011, after learning the art of upholstery while attending automotive trade school in Wyoming. With his wife, Chelsea, and numerous dedicated employees, he is bringing back the art of upholstering and heirloom-quality restoration to the city of Portland, Oregon. Revive Upholstery & Design is just one example of the resurgent artisan and trade communities that are appearing throughout the country.

Terry Hancock and his wife wanted to create a legacy for their family. When he and his father, Gary, shut down their Oregon lumber company in 1993, they used the wood from the old truss bow lumber warehouse building to build an oceanfront home in Oregon. With the help of architect Nathan Good, they created a home by reusing all the reclaimed beams, planks, and trusses that came out of the old building. The walls themselves, where you can see the old bolt holes, speak to the past, reminding their kids and their grandchildren where their family came from. Their history lives on in their new home.

Supporting an Artisanal Revival

Tradespeople are vital to our communities and our small industries. As an interior designer, I'm finding it harder and harder to find quality craftspeople and tradespeople to work with. Parents are no longer proudly passing down their trade expertise to their children, due to lack of interest or time, and trade schools have been closing. But we can encourage our school leaders, parents, and grandparents to help preserve these skills and trades, and create great job opportunities in fields like welding, electrical, plumbing, painting, tilework, and upholstering. By purchasing items made by these artisans, we can support the revival of these amazing craftsmen and do

The designers at Make King created a simple background of square tile, dark grout, and white walls in the basement mudroom entrance of their Mount Tabor, Oregon, renovation project. To liven up the palette, they added a large reclaimed-wood beam bench and a coatrack made from more salvaged wood, giving the space just the right amount of warmth. The midcentury vintage light was given an update by the designers themselves. Lizzy and Luis, the homeowners, then only had to add a vintage rug and a few other details to make a perfect place for their dog, Pippa, to hang out.

our part to champion these trades in our communities.

Rethinking How We Buy and Design Homes

Once upon a time, folks would just put unwanted, broken, or old stuff in the dumpster. But today folks are either calling rebuild centers to pick up these items, giving away older furniture, or opening up to the idea of reusing pieces. I'm honored to work with clients on residential and commercial design projects, such as boutique motels, resorts, inns, hotels, restaurants, and offices. The builders, contractors, and vendors I work with are now seeing that reusing and building with reclaimed materials is not as complicated as once thought. These owners, managers, and employees are looking at things differently now, and as a result they are actively searching the grounds of their properties for treasures, looking for ways to reuse what they already have, and taking the time to recycle and donate the materials and furnishings they're no longer using. It only takes a little bit of encouragement to help folks take that small first step on the path of designing and discarding in a mindful way, and most people are excited and happy to do it. I like to believe that I have not only helped create unique and beautiful designs but have also changed the mindset of my clients.

I'm seeing another amazing trend with homeowners who are asking their architects and builders to incorporate vintage, salvaged, and recycled materials into their designs. Homebuyers are also seeking out builders and designers who have already used this process in renovated houses that were subsequently put on the market. In other words, buyers are looking for new and renovated homes that have character already built in. Many homeowners don't want to do the renovation themselves—they just don't have the time or inclination— but it doesn't mean they don't want the character that comes with things like recycled tile backsplashes or vintage double drainboard sinks. Potential homeowners now want to see these pieces in the houses they view.

Left: This farmhouse-style kitchen, belonging to George and Rachael Ramos, in Portland, Oregon, is filled with gorgeous custom cabinetry, natural light, and vintage finds. George Ramos, a cabinetmaker, built his own kitchen cabinets out of reclaimed Douglas fir from the old Port Authority Building in Portland. People typically assume that by using reclaimed wood, the finished product will look rustic, old, or "country," but this stunning modern kitchen proves that using reclaimed materials can be done in a way that feels contemporary and clean.

Right: This bathroom was designed by Shannon Quimby, a designer and stylist well known for her salvage and recycling efforts, including the REX (reuse everything experiment) Project in Portland, Oregon. This bathroom incorporates recycled materials into new products and fixtures, such as the recycled glass aggregate in a new concrete countertop, and the new wall tiles, made from recycled glass and porcelain. Vintage green glass doorknobs have been added as handles on this custom-built, reclaimed-wood vanity to create a pleasing recycled-but-new design. Other vintage touches, such as the mirror, painting, and lighting, give this room a modern bohemian feel.

For Profit—For Planet—For People

A lot of folks think that you can't have a for-profit company that also takes care of people and the planet. Well, that's just not the case. Many companies I work with provide amazing products in a mindful way while still bringing in the bacon. And we are not just talking mom-and-pop companies. Even bigwigs like large carpet, furniture, bedding, tile, and glassware companies are recognizing the value of doing business this way. Make a list of

When Removing Your Own Things

WHETHER YOU'RE SPRING CLEANING, RENOVATING, OR MOVING, SOMETIMES THINGS HAVE TO GO. There are so many places you can send them besides the landfill. If you want to try to make some money, then try selling them on your local Front Porch Forum or Craigslist. (If I'm selling something online, I always ask potential buyers to contact me with their email and phone number—scammers are not willing to do that.) If it is a vintage piece or an antique, I reach out to my local architectural and vintage shops, because they are always looking to buy such items. Send them a picture and ask them what they would pay for it. I bring a lot of items (sinks, cabinets, stoves, countertops, and other fixtures and finishes) to my local rebuild centers. When we bought our cottage on the lake, we lived in it for two years before we could afford to rebuild. Once we were ready, we hired the local nonprofit rebuild center to deconstruct the cottage, piece by piece. They removed everything, from porches to insulation, and recycled them. They even took the nails out of the wood and reclaimed the old wood pieces. Not only did we feel great that all these materials would be reused, we also knew this deconstruction was a job training program that taught people the construction trade. It was a win, win, win all around.

Emily and Calvin Sellers bought their home in Carmine, Texas, from antique dealers, so it was already full of character. They loved all the old fixtures, the reclaimed-wood walls, and the recycled details throughout the home. They made the living spaces their own by adding their personal vintage furniture and family pieces. Finding a home that already had been creatively renovated using previously loved pieces was something they were searching for, and they were thrilled when they found it.

Prince Coffee is part of the Revive Studio space in Portland. With a great copper countertop (copper mills use 95 percent recycled materials for copper sheets and save 85 percent of the energy needed for new production), hand-built bar, and local art on the wall (my favorite is *Bigfoot*, created by Karen Wippich), it's both an intimate barista space and a perfect backdrop for some of Revive's recent design work. These reupholstered 1960s bar stools that Leland's dad found in Wyoming feature felted wool from Denmark, sumptuous leather, and nickel upholstery nails. Their hip, modern look is perfect for the coffee shop, or for a home bar or kitchen island. These types of beneficial partnerships are becoming more common.

Lizzy and Luis's master bathroom, designed by Chelsea and Brandt Kaemingk, of the design company Make King, in Portland, Oregon, has a just-right combination of clean lines, warm tones, and modern tile work. Lots of natural light and the use of a beautifully detailed vintage piece such as the vanity they picked up at Stars Antiques Mall in Sellwood, Oregon, gives the bathroom a welcoming feeling. The contrast of modern vessel sink and vintage brass faucet is a master class in mixing traditional and modern. A neutral base was created through soft tone tiles and wall colors, allowing the wood furniture to stand out as the room's centerpiece. Chelsea and Brandt are known for their home renovations that combine high-end vintage materials and custom products they make to order (fixtures and lighting), and new clean-lined materials.

products you need, and then search for providers that use recycled materials, practice fair trade, pay fair wages, are sustainable, and do well by the quality of their products and guarantees. Granted, you may not hit it out of the ballpark every time, but as consumers we can make companies stand up and take notice of who we're purchasing from, and why.

Take, for instance, Fireclay. I started to use Fireclay's tile products because I liked their reuse of old porcelain toilets, which, no longer water efficient, are being recycled. How fun is that! The reuse of toilets piqued my interest in this company, but I love their whole story. They started out small, going from place to place in a time-consuming search for materials they could recycle and use in their tiles. Today, they work closely with the community and use more than 70 percent recycled materials in their Debris Series, which features some of the most sustainable ceramic tile in the world. They also recycle old sinks, porcelain scraps, waste glass, granite dust, and other goodies. As the love for recycled products grows, so does their company and the variety of product lines they sell. This type of recycling is redefining the industry, one tile at a time.

Your One-of-a-Kind Piece: Rare, Beautiful, and Distinct

If my house were on fire, I know there are only a couple of things I would grab (after my family, of course), and one is a beautiful old painting given to me by my dearest friend, Marty Rudolph. I started working for her as a college intern when I was 19 years old, and we've been friends ever since. There was a painting that hung in her house, and I admired it so. This year, a package arrived at my house, and it was the old painting. She had moved into a new home and no longer had a place for it. But she knew that I would cherish the piece as much as she did. It is these special vintage, antique, and heirloom pieces that bring distinction and fond memories to our homes. You don't need many. Find something of value (not necessarily monetary—but emotional) that you and your family can appreciate and admire and that you can pass down,

Redecorating and designing the 74 charming cottages at the historic resort of Basin Harbor, on the shores of Lake Champlain, in Vermont, over the past few years has been a lot of fun for me. A bar area in one of the cottages has been painted a modern dark blue, and the vintage buoy I found goes great with the new pendant light. Keeping the decor simple, yet bold, lets your oldie-but-goodies take center stage, no matter the style, whether it is rustic, contemporary, retro, or modern. We have many more cottages to design, and I'm thrilled to be scouring the resort's numerous attics, barns, and closets for more fun finds to bring back into their public spaces and lodging rooms.

knowing that it will be loved for many years to come. When you appreciate something of significance, other things that have little importance become less of an obsession or need.

All in the Family

Many salvage shops, booths at flea markets and antique fairs, and vintage shops are family-run businesses. It's not uncommon to see husbands and wives, sisters and brothers, working side by side at an antique fair. It's a way of life for many, and they provide us with recycled materials, antique furnishings, and vintage goods. So when you buy that old plate or vintage sofa at these places, remember that you're supporting a family and the family business.

Bringing You Joy

After years of speaking with people across the nation about recycled, vintage, and salvaged goods, I can tell you these items bring joy, subconsciously as well as consciously. We all know the joy we feel when we find the perfect vintage piece, or when we find an old treasure in the attic that had long ago been given up for lost. But there's also the unexplained happiness we feel when we are in certain spaces—we're not sure where it's coming from, but we're sure it's there. A house that feels soulless can be transformed

Tricia Rose's Californian home is filled with found objects from the ocean and elsewhere. Pillows made from scrap pieces of fabric from her Rough Linen company complement vintage throws. The antique luggage basket, once used on trains crossing the Scottish and English countryside, serves as the couch's end table. For Tricia, this piece brings back fond memories of her childhood in England. The DIY mirror is made with driftwood pieces she found in the water in front of their cottage. It's details like these that bring snippets of joyful memories into our homes. Taking pride in pieces we've created makes our homes unique to us.

through the addition of treasured pieces and age-old materials, as they carry on their own history and joy. And I've talked to dozens and dozens of people who feel the same way. It might sound a bit out there, but they understand and appreciate the soul that comes with reclaimed materials and decor.

When you walk into a home that feels comfortable, warm, and inviting, take the time to see what it is about it that you love. Is it the cozy recovered couch, the unique vintage mirror, the family heirlooms, the textures, the textiles? Whatever you identify, use your newfound knowledge to bring items that have meaning and purpose to you into your own home and use them to create conscious and subconscious joy.

Heather and Andrew Lynds' kitchen was once a storage shed built off the back of a late 1700s farmhouse in Vermont, part of the Mad River Barn property. When they renovated, they asked me to help. To make the room feel bigger than it was, I gave it a large open area with the farmhouse table in the middle of the space. My friend and neighbor, Brett Bundock, built the table using reclaimed porch post legs from Mason Brothers Architectural Salvage Warehouse (in Essex Junction, Vermont), and wood that was salvaged during the renovation project and set aside for future use. The countertops are made from old schoolhouse chalkboards, found at Vermont Salvage Exchange, in White River Junction, Vermont, and the wood on the hood vent is reclaimed from the renovation. With low windows that go right up to the counter and reclaimed-wood open shelving, this small storage shed has been transformed into a light and airy modern farmhouse kitchen.

3

The Joy of the Search

Searches, Treasures, and Finds

By now you're probably so excited about designing and decorating with vintage and reclaimed materials that you're chomping at the bit and ready to head out! But before you go, I'd like to give you some tips for your travels. People always ask me whether I design with vintage and salvage in mind, or if I find a vintage or recycled piece and design around it. The answer is both, and frankly, it's the best part of my job. I'm always open-minded about what will come my way. You just have to look at things differently. Here are some ways you can do just that.

For the design of the Longhouse bathrooms at Mad River Barn, I combined vintage and salvaged materials with new materials that work for this bustling business. A local craftsman made the vanities using reclaimed lumber (true 2" × 4"s) and vintage sinks found at ReSource Building Material Store, in Burlington, Vermont. I added layers of black and white paint, sanded off much of it, and then sealed it well. With the addition of simple subway tiling, new ceramic flooring, and a modern mirror to show off the vintage turkey feeders I picked up at a Country Living Fair (which were turned into light fixtures by Conant Metal & Light), this guest bathroom space is unlike any you've seen before.

This wall sconce plug-in light fixture was a DIY project I did with my husband, Steve. I picked a couple of old ceiling fixtures and took the guts out of them. We ordered the plug-in with switch set online (we had to take it apart a little to fit it through the hole). I sanded down the brass and taped up the glass, and then sprayed the brass fixture with silver paint. Then I peeled the tape off the glass and sprayed it with a paint that gave a mercury glass effect. I wiped a little off to give it an antiqued look. Voilà! Instant romance.

Practice Makes Perfect

Train yourself to look at things differently. Check out items that you don't have a specific purpose for, and then ask yourself a simple question: "What are three things I could do with that?" For example, an old drawer from a dresser could become a dog bed or a wall hanging for books or a display for the middle of a dining table filled with glass vases and flowers. You could even add wheels and slide it under your bed. Do you see where I'm going? You'll become less overwhelmed by all the stuff you come across in a shop if you just take your time to focus on the individual pieces rather than the whole space.

Know Your Neighbors

Get to know your local recycle centers, antique shops, secondhand stores, architectural salvage shops, and rebuilding centers. Know where your rebuild center is and what they usually carry, where your closest architectural salvage shop is, and the flea markets and antique shows in your area. You may not be able to get to them all the time, but it's important to swing by periodically and get the lay of the land. That

This ornament collection I saw at the Barge Canal Market in Burlington, Vermont, is a great example of design inspiration. Husband and wife team Jeremy Smith and Adele Lawrence do an amazing job on their displays, and it's fun to browse through their warehouse space filled with midcentury finds and stylish goodies. This wall display would also look great in a bedroom with black and white family photos or in a cottage with a chain of old fishing hooks or in an urban setting, like a modern industrial style loft, with a crisp white wall and old locks. What else can you see displayed in this way?

way, when you see an amazing piece for a sweet price, you can make an informed decision about it. Plus, as you know, at these types of shops the materials they carry changes every day, depending on what they are deconstructing at the moment, or what's been donated or sold to them directly.

Carry a List

Having a list helps, especially with measurements. What do you want in your living room, bathroom, or bedroom? Couches, chairs, maybe some architectural beams? Carry your list and a tape measure with you at all times. That way, if you see something you love you can grab it; these materials and furnishings are unique, not mass produced, and so once an item is gone, it's gone. When I'm near a shop I like, I zip in, take out my list, and do a quick walk-through. Say hello to the shopkeeper and just see what's there. Since it's reclaimed and vintage stuff, it's never the same, day to day.

If you're anything like me, half the fun is in the search. You never know what you may find and where, and lists can enhance the enjoyment of your hunt. For example, I've been collecting old Nancy Drew and Hardy Boys books since my daughter was born. I carry a tattered list with me of the books I'm missing. If I'm traveling and happen to pass by a secondhand bookstore or flea market, I make a stop, pull out the list, and search for the missing titles. I'm talking 17 years of searching!

Obviously, it would be much easier (and faster) if I just sat down at my computer and ordered them off a secondhand site, but where's the fun in that? The search—the find—the score—the adding of it to the collection—that's adventure. So have a plan, keep your eyes open, but don't be in such a hurry that you miss out on all the enjoyment of the journey, because it's part of the story of your home decor.

Don't Be Afraid to Ask

At this point, for better or worse, most of the people at all my local vintage and secondhand shops, rebuild centers, and architectural salvage locations know me. So when I stop in or call them to ask for a specific item,

I gave a presentation as part of the Fifth Third Bank's Women's Design Series, held at the Sarasota Architectural Salvage, in Sarasota, Florida. Not only was it a blast to speak to this great group of women about working with vintage and salvaged materials, but it was also fun to look around the salvage shop and see what they had. In the backyard, I saw two items that would make incredible design pieces. Seeing things differently comes in handy at the most unexpected moments. The round metal piece I would use as a coffee table in a modern home. Add a gorgeous glass top and it would be stunning. The large letter S would be perfect filled with living plants and placed in a sunny dining room or kitchen space (filled with herbs). Can't you just picture these pieces now?

Finding the right light fixtures in a sea of vintage and recycled pieces takes a little bit of imagination. If you're not comfortable with rewiring, you can get someone to do it for you for around $40–$100, depending on the light fixture. I liked the shape of these two vintage ceiling fixtures I saw at ReSource Building Material Store, in Burlington, Vermont. After removing the insides, painting, and adding plug-ins, these fixtures were transformed.

they're pretty responsive to checking or keeping an eye out for me. Let these folks know what you're looking for. It never hurts.

Tweak Your Idea

Again, salvaged materials and vintage finds may not come in the exact size you're looking for, but is it close enough? Or can you change your design slightly to fit the perfect piece you found? I'm always a little bit flexible in my designs when it comes to using old stuff. Designing is a fluid process, especially when it comes to using reclaimed pieces. I've been known to cut legs down on a table to turn it into a coffee table, or to add legs or wheels to bring a table up higher. I've done the same to bring a dresser up to counter height to serve as an island, and have even added trim to the edges of doors to create that perfect fit for a barn door slider.

Does It Measure Up?

Make sure you have the right measurements for what you need. I can't tell you how many dressers I have to look at before I find the perfect one for my needs. Let's say, for example, I want to drop a sink into

I have a hard time passing up old glass knobs and broken vintage jewelry. When I've gathered enough of them, I have an ornament-making party and everyone gets to go home with their very own vintage glass costume jewelry holiday ornament. All you need is some stiff wire, wire cutters, old costume jewelry, some crystal pieces from old chandeliers, some vintage glass knobs (with holes all the way through), and a gaggle of friends with a willingness to try something new. I find these in bins at architectural salvage shops, antique stores, or at antique fairs. I always ask if they have these smaller pieces (broken or not). Many times, they'll have a box of these things lying around somewhere. I don't mind chips or if a faux pearl or two is missing. These would also make some excellent curtain tie-backs and dream catchers.

after

before

one. First, I need to make sure I won't be cutting into a valuable piece. Then I have to measure the dresser to be sure that the hole I want to cut will not damage the structural integrity of the furniture piece. You know the rule: measure twice, cut once!

Keep Old Blankets in Your Car

Let's say someone hands you a free cast-iron vintage sink from their basement and it's beyond grimy. You can't say no—it's free! Or let's say you're out and about and find a great stack of wood or a pile of drawer pulls, but they're pretty dirty. In both cases, you want the items but worry about what the dirt and grime will do to your car. This won't be an issue if you pack a pile of blankets in your car for just such occasions. Like a good scout, always be prepared.

It didn't take much to liven up this 1980s living room for my client in ski country. Using dimensional lumber (again, most likely found at your rebuild centers), we created a built-in book system around the gas fireplace. Gathering books is easy—you can buy them in bulk at your library book sale (usually only once a year, so put it on your calendar), or you can look online at sites that sell secondhand books by the subject, color, pound, and type (hardcover or paperback). The coffee table came from a secondhand shop, and I wrapped the top in a piece of metal I found at the scrap yard. This design detail is a simple way to bring depth, texture, and color into your living room.

Look for Design Inspiration

When I'm shopping for vintage and repurposed goods, I don't just go looking for the purchase; I take the time to see how different shops display their items. Some of my best ideas come from seeing the unique ways things are put out for sale, especially at vintage fairs and specialty boutiques.

Understand Quality

Get a feel for pieces of furniture. Does that old desk give you the quality and look that you want, and will it stand the test of time? Is it solid wood, does it have a veneer, can you identify the brand or name, and is it stapled together or does it have dovetailed joints? Does the rug have layers of dog hair—and if so, can it be cleaned? Does the trunk have mold on it? Some of these issues can be taken care of, and some are red flags. If you want to paint an item or fix it up, then make sure it's a solid piece and worth your time. If you're using something for a structural purpose, such as a beam, or something that has to be up to code (a lighting fixture or bricks near fireplaces), make sure the items are up to snuff. Working with

after

This dining room wall was covered with pine reclaimed from a barn. I picked up the wood at a rebuild center in central Vermont. I asked the installers to place them on the wall in a diagonal pattern. Then they were whitewashed, which totally brightened up the room while letting the character of the old wood shine through. The chairs were found at Habitat for Humanity and arranged around a custom-made farmhouse table, built with reclaimed porch posts and wood. With finishing touches like the antique rug found at Champlain Valley Antique Center, in Shelburne, Vermont, and a modern light fixture picked up at the local Stowe Kitchen Bath & Linens store, the chic space is almost unrecognizable from the outdated townhouse dining room it was before.

before

These textiles are just a couple of the thousands that Wendy Lewis of The Textile Trunk has collected over the years. Wendy searches for beautiful pieces around the world and then sells them online and at big antique shows, such as Brimfield. She helps folks who are looking for specific pieces, whether it's for curtains, upholstery, bedding, or more. Take advantage of the experts around you. There are folks who know about textiles, wood, cast-iron fixtures, lighting, artwork, ceramic bowls, pottery, belts, banners, signs, you name it. There's an expert for everything; you just have to find them.

experienced companies that have a good understanding of your needs is a best practice. Moreover, these experts can tell you where you can go to bring a vintage item up to code.

Ask the Builder, Carpenter, or Tradesperson

If you are unsure about a piece or idea and you have a good relationship with someone with a trade skill that pertains to your item, then by all means get their input. It's important that you get a handle on the costs of your project, especially any additional labor fees. Old doors are gorgeous, but they may need a custom door frame. Old hardware is fun to use, but using it may require a special screw to keep it in place. No matter how manageable the task may seem, you should not go into a project without understanding the amount of work, time, and money that adding reclaimed materials will bring to your construction project.

Give Yourself a Reality Check

I love a lot of different styles. One day I could be a bohemian hippy, the next a cowgirl, the next a sexy modern Cosmo girl (okay—this is all

An old piece of wood that I picked up at Mason Brothers Architectural Salvage was put on brackets to create an instant entranceway desk. This mini-office uses very little space and has a modern farmhouse feel.

Tying it all together, an antique wood door from the ReSource Building Material Store, painted a bright red, totally changes up the entrance of this once outdated Vermont townhouse. When you walk in and see a gorgeous vintage door with tons of character painted bright red, you know you're in for a fun time.

Carol and Randy Dupree's old warehouse-turned-home is plenty big enough to fill with colorful and fun finds. A company at the mall was throwing away a chandelier and the Duprees asked if they could have it. They found the chairs at Goodwill (they were originally pink vinyl, but the Duprees transformed them with some paint and reupholstery work using fabric they picked up at the Bluebird Auction). When they visited a furniture consignment store in Palm Beach, Florida, they spied the extra-large antique English table that had once been a foyer table. The owner of the store said that the 12' × 6" table was too big for most people's homes, but not Carol and Randy's large warehouse. A friend found the ticket sign lying in the grass and weeds at an old racecar track, which they took home, cleaned up, and hung. The colorful vintage rug actually serves as both a window curtain (on a large metal swing arm) and as a decorative hanging. Together, these bold and heavy pieces work well in the large brick-walled space.

These suitcases were a gift from my friend Regina, who knew I would love them. I picked up the old metal baker's rack for $20 at Burnett Scrap Metals, in Hinesburg, Vermont (a metal scrap yard I drop by every once in a while with a plate of homemade cookies for the folks). Cutting thick reclaimed wood for shelving, I created an instant clothing rack. This kind of storage display is practical for apartments, tiny houses, and retail shops that want a place to store things while looking cool at the same time. In addition to racks, old country store bins, mechanic carts, and industrial metal storage units are all good options, depending on the look and feel you want.

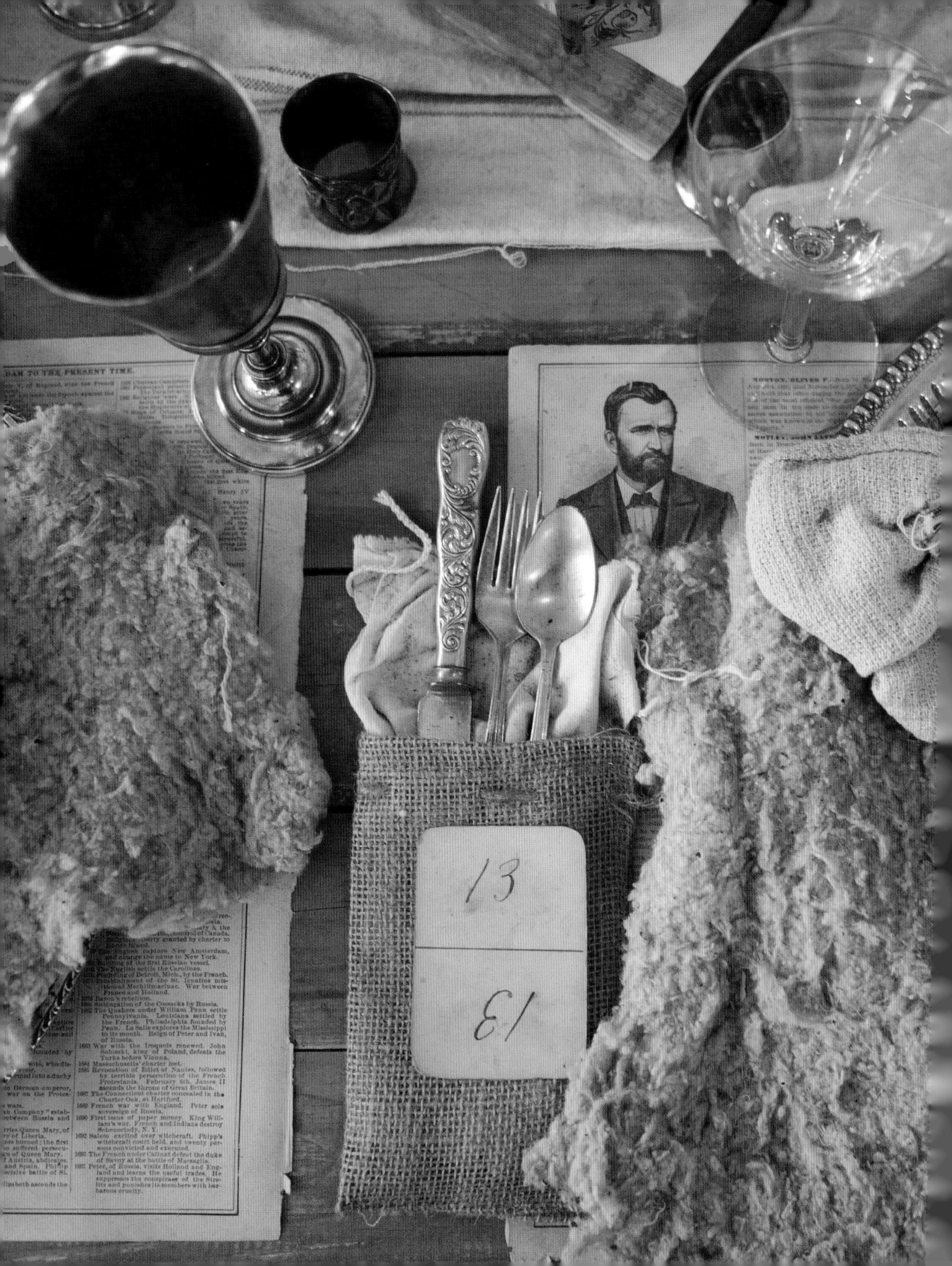

Karen and Patrick Kenny and their daughter, Bonnie, of South Porch Antiques, don't have a storefront. Instead, they do all their selling at vintage and antique fairs, and they know how to display! Karen is especially good at creating dishware and table settings. You can get a number of table setting ideas from the many displays in their booth. This one includes vintage paper as placemats, stoneware bowls, pieces of raw cotton, scraps of ticking and old linens used as napkins, antique silver goblets, burlap silverware holders, vintage silver, and more. Alone, each one of these would be interesting, but together, they're stunning. The more you look, the more you'll find ideas for your own displays, table settings, and decor.

in my mind, of course). But the fact is, even though I like a lot of design styles, I don't have them all in my house. Sometimes, I just need to say no to myself, understanding that not every cool piece can fit with my home decor. That said, I've been known to bring stuff home and hide it in the carport out back in the hopes that one day it will fit, or a client will love it as much as I do. When considering a new piece, take a deep breath and ask yourself the tough questions: Does it go with my decor and style? Is it the right size? Will the rest of my family like it? Is it something I can't live without?

Places to Search

When hunting for pieces and materials, the most obvious stops are antique shops, salvage yards, rebuild centers, recycle centers, nonprofit secondhand shops, garage sales, and antique and vintage fairs. All are easy enough to find and utilize. Even some mass-merchandise brick-and-mortar shops are now carrying recycled and vintage pieces. But there are other places to watch out for and think about that may not yet be on your radar:

- University/college warehouse sales
- Hotel sales
- Auctions
- Library sales
- Scrap metal yards
- Used office furniture shops
- Carpet stores (for remnant pieces)
- Used restaurant suppliers
- Secondhand appliance stores
- Furniture stores (for fabric and leather sample books)
- Recycle centers
- Mechanic shops
- Secondhand plumbing supply shops
- Wallpaper and carpet stores (for wallpaper books and carpet samples)

Once you start the search, one location will lead you to another location, and then another, and then you'll find out about another secret spot, and then. . . . The adventures can run far and wide, especially if you ask the salespeople about *their* favorite places to go.

Looking Online

I could write an entire book on places online where you can find secondhand stuff. Simply stated,

Above: I'm a huge fan of maps. I try to put them in many of my design projects, because I'd like to believe everyone else is as enamored with them as I am. When I see them at fairs, here at the Country Living Fair in Atlanta, for example, I snap them up. You can hang them in an office, above a bed, in a dining room, a bathroom, or wherever you need an affordable bold statement. Just make sure it's easy to access, because people tend to like to get up close and personal to look at maps.

Right: In this office space, I reused the owner's chairs. The table was built out of reclaimed live edge wood (the edge of the wood is left in its natural state) and an old car rack I picked up at the Barge Canal Market to use as the base. With a vintage desk lamp, an old map, and maple buckets I got at Champlain Valley Antique Center, in Shelburne, Vermont, HMC Advertising's meeting room is as creative as their team.

This 2" × 15" piece of Douglas fir was picked out by a homeowner. In this case, the wood is sold by the linear foot and was ready to be picked up. These were once ceiling joists in an old building. Now they're used for benches, shelving, counters, entertainment centers, and tables. The salvaged wood on the left has been milled and edged, and then strapped in bundles. It is ready for an easy install of a shiplap-style wall.

some of the first places you should try are free online community-based sites, such as Front Porch Forum and Craigslist. Even your Facebook page has a shopping section where you can find people around you who are listing things for sale. If you can't find what you need within a few miles of your home, expand the scope of your online search using keywords such as: *architectural, salvage shop, reclaimed wood, vintage sinks, salvaged doors, used building supplies, secondhand furniture*, or whatever you're looking for.

Wood . . . n't You Know

Why do I count wood as a separate treasure? Because wood is by far the most available reclaimed material today. Old buildings, felled trees, paneling, subflooring, dimensional lumber (2" × 4"s, 1" × 4"s, etc.), siding, trusses, beams, floorboards,

The live edge (the natural wood is left on the edge) slabs, shown here at Salvage Works, are the most recently urban salvaged trees in the Portland area. To see what is available in your hometown, you can check with your city's parks department and find out what they do with felled trees. These reclaimed pieces are the real deal and the old-growth character is not something you can re-create artificially.

balusters, stair treads, doors, trim . . . the list goes on, and the uses for this material are endless. Understanding these materials will help you determine the best way you can use them in your home.

Types of Reclaimed Wood

When people use the word *reclaim*, they are usually referring to wood, particularly antique wood, vintage wood, and secondhand dimensional lumber. Reclaimed wood can be urban salvaged (old rare trees that have fallen down or had to be removed due to other issues), sinker salvage (logs dragged up from the bottom of rivers and lakes), antique and heritage lumber (dismantlings from old buildings, when a 2" × 4" really meant a 2" × 4"), and secondhand dimensional lumber (also called

At Salvage Works, in Portland, Oregon, Rachel and Preston Browning are more than happy to help you find the perfect wood for your project. Their backyard is where the wood is processed. The pile in the back is fencing from all over Portland—it has a great gray hue that is a popular color. The beams in the front are from a 1950s warehouse in Portland. The Douglas fir sheathing (behind the beams) is from a 1930s house in Milwaukie, Oregon. And the barn wood (under the blue tarp) is pine from a turn-of-the-century barn in Bend, Oregon. So many types of wood from many locations, buildings, and ages end up in this yard. It's here that all the surface nails are removed. The wood is then moved into the warehouse to be sold to the general public—homeowners, artisans, builders, designers, restaurant owners, all those folks who love the history, look, and feel of salvaged reclaimed wood.

Wood Verbiage

LIGHT SKIP: Only goes through the planer once, which creates a rough-finish look that keeps the character of the material, including the original mill marks and the patina.

HEAVY SKIP: Goes through the planer more than once, which creates a less rough look while retaining a rough finish. This process brings out more of the natural bright color while still keeping some of the character and patina.

CLEAN MILL: Removes all of the patina and creates a smooth, clean finish.

nominal, which is a modern 2" × 4" that is really a $1^{1}/_{2}$" × $3^{1}/_{2}$" and is usually found at a rebuild center). And this is just the tip of the iceberg.

Don't Judge by Its Cover

Most old wood will be brown, gray, or very dark because of oxidation, dust, and dirt. If you're looking for wood, always carry some sandpaper and water. That way you can sand a small piece of the wood to give you an idea of its natural color once planed or sanded down. Then you can pour some water on the sanded piece to see what it will look like if it is sealed with polyurethane, wax, or some other type of sealer. Even if you're going to whitewash or paint the wood, it will still need a sanding to get all the grime and dirt off so that your stain, paint, shellac, Osmo (a European eco-friendly product line of oil- and wax-based finishes), or other finish will adhere.

Shopping for Wood

At architectural salvage shops and reclaimed wood shops, you just have to shop the aisles, like at your local grocery store. You walk in, pick out some things, and walk out. Shopping for salvaged wood is not as hard as many believe.

Once you get to know your local vintage shops, you'll get an idea of what each of them specializes in, or at least leans toward in their finds. The Barge Canal Market, in Burlington, Vermont, tends to have a lot of midcentury furniture. That doesn't mean they don't carry a wide selection of other goodies, including an old wooden canoe and a ton of vintage paper prints. I've said it before and I'll say it again—visit these stores often because they will always have something new on offer.

This reclaimed Douglas fir table, in the Salvage Works showroom, has what's called a light skip finish (it's only been through a planer once, which maintains more of the character of the wood). With a botanical succulent and industrial vintage lamp, it's just the right look for any loft apartment or industrial-styled home.

Be Flexible

Rachel Browning of Salvage Works, located in Portland, Oregon, and I share the same advice when working with reclaimed wood: Be flexible. Every barn, building, and structure is different. Even on the same structure, pieces will vary depending on whether they were north- or south-facing, or on the windy side. Be open to what is available. If you have a specific type of reclaimed wood in mind, be willing to wait or search it out. In new-product catalogs all things are the same, but it's not like that in the old wood business. If you see something you love, buy it, because what's in the retail shop today may be totally different tomorrow.

Unique Local Wood

Urban salvage, sometimes called felled wood (fallen urban lumber), is reactive salvaging. That is, these are trees in a city or town that require removal due to storm damage, rot, disease, building construction, or roads. Many of these trees are exotic species planted 50 to 100 years ago that today are really hard to come by. This urban salvaged wood is rare and not actively cut elsewhere. There are even companies, like the brother team of

The pantry door made from reclaimed wood that came from the renovation project itself is a great example of a usable design piece that also saves space (no swinging door). Heather and Andrew Lynds' shed-turned-kitchen is filled with design details that speak to the history of the old home. We left the original 1700s farmhouse wall exposed on the left-hand side of the kitchen and framed out a modern trimmed opening to the living room, carefully mixing old features with new design.

City Bench, located in Higganum, Connecticut, that work solely with urban trees. They give each one of their furniture and custom pieces a birth certificate describing the source tree's origin, its significance in the town it came from, and the story behind it. I'm thrilled to see more and more communities, cities,

and towns making an effort to save the unique species of felled trees in their urban areas instead of just chipping them up. You can do a search for these types of trees in your area through your city's forest service or maintenance department. It's possible that they already have a relationship with artisans and salvage yards. Then find those artisans and yards and see what they have. Check often, because the types of trees they will have at any given moment will change.

You Say Po-ta-to, I Say Po-tah-to

Every place that sells wood is affected by where it's located, what type of store it is, and who they sell to. This is truly the case in the business of reclaimed wood. There is no right or wrong way to do it—but if you don't understand the pricing model a particular business uses, you could be in for a big surprise when the bill comes in.

A board foot is a measurement of volume. By definition, a board foot is 1 square foot by 1 inch thick. But some places just sell it by the square foot and bypass the thickness of the wood. Other places just sell by

If you're willing to do a little work, things can come together, like this guest bedroom at Mad River Barn, in Waitsfield, Vermont. The tables are made from scrap pieces of stone I picked up at my local stone company. The 2" × 4"s came from a rebuild center, and the headboard wood came from the project itself, as well as another client who was selling barn wood. The pillows are made from the old wool blankets that used to be on the beds, the table lamp was custom made by Conant Metal & Light from pieces of an old floor lamp, and the blanket on the bed is made from recycled sari cloth by Dignify.

the linear foot, which means they consider the length of the board but don't take into account the width. When in doubt, ask.

When I'm Looking for Wood

Depending on what I need the wood for will decide where I will go first. For wall paneling and flooring, I pay a visit to architectural salvage shops. They will have already culled out the wood that is damaged or structurally unsound for my uses. Also, I rely heavily on their expertise about the wood, how much of it I will need, and how I can clean, sand, and finish it for the best look possible. Many of these shops will prep the wood for me, and even give it a light cleaning.

When I want the wood to be ready to go, cleaned, planed, and even sanded, I will go straight to reclaimed lumber shops that specialize in just that. When

This renovation project by the designers at Make King, in the Alberta neighborhood in Portland, Oregon, is a perfect example of how to use reclaimed wood in its natural state while creating a cozy and comfortable modern home. Using reclaimed old-growth Douglas fir for the walls, ceiling, benches, and floors gives the space a clean look. A different treatment was used on the floor than on the wood surround. The wood came from Salvage Works and was actually milled from glulam beams salvaged from an old commercial building. The bold space needed bold fixtures, and the designers did a great job by creating an extra-large zinc-topped table and drum shade light. This space plays a huge role in this small home, and it's more than just a dining table for Michael, Michelle, and their family. It's also a place for parties, card games, reading, enjoying midnight snacks, work, and for Madison, the dog, it's practically his very own clubhouse.

searching for a reclaimed lumber store, it's best to get a reference for the company from a designer or architect who has used their products before. Using ready-to-go wood will cost more in terms of the actual material, but it will cost you less in labor. This is because the wood will be ready for you to install and you won't have to do all the prep work that sometimes comes with working with reclaimed wood. You can ask for samples (samples are free or cost a nominal fee) so that you can see what type of reclaimed wood and finish will work best for your project.

If I have plenty of time but a tight budget, I'll go to my local rebuild center and ask if they have any deconstruction projects coming up. Oftentimes, you can get a large quantity of wood this way, but it may not be in perfect condition. If you're willing to do a little prep work, this can be an affordable solution.

Consider not only your budget, but the quality of wood you need and what you'll need to do to get it ready. Really understand the look you're going for from your reclaimed wood, because if you are taking the time to use reclaimed lumber, then the look and feel is very important and it's worth the extra effort to get it right.

Painted Options

There is so much to know about reclaimed wood—whether it is heritage lumber (full dimensional, when a 2" × 4" is actually a 2" × 4") or nominal lumber (today's modern 2" × 4", which is actually a $1^{1}/_{2}$" × $3^{1}/_{2}$"). Regardless, you should be aware that if it's painted, and especially if it was painted before the late 1970s, it may contain lead paint. The potential presence of lead is not a deal breaker. Just follow the EPA's Lead Renovation, Repair, and Painting (RRP) Rule that can be found online.

How to Measure a Board:
Linear Versus Board Foot Versus Square Foot

WHY DOES THIS MATTER, YOU ASK? Because if you're buying a lot of wood, understanding these differences will save you a lot of money. So pay attention.

LINEAR FOOT: Only the length of the board is considered. When paying by linear foot, the width of a board is not considered. For example, if a board is $5 per linear foot and you're buying a board that is 5 feet long, then you will pay $25.

SQUARE FOOT: The area of the board sets the price. If a board is $5 per square foot and the width of the board is 6", then for a foot (length) of that board will cost $2.50. If the width of the board is 18", then a foot (length) of that board will cost $7.50.

BOARD FOOT: Multiply by the thickness of a board and then divide by the cubic inch of its thickness. (For example, a 1"-thick board that is 12" long by 12" wide is one board foot, and 144 cubic inches. Similarly, a 2"-thick board that is 6" wide by 12" long is also one board foot and 144 cubic inches.) Online calculators for board foot measurements are a terrific resource. If you find boards with ends that are not usable (because of rot, breakage, or any number of other reasons) ask the seller if the unusable portions are included in the measurements. If you're buying 10,000 square feet of wood, it adds up. Also, make sure to get extra wood for your project for this exact reason. You don't want to run out of the reclaimed wood by a mere few feet, since finding the same color, wear, and look will be almost impossible once that specific batch is gone.

I had some serious fun with these doll head planters, made by Tim Brock, master craftsman at Salvage Works. Gathering the creative planters from all over the shop, I used them together to invent a fun table display. You could even make an entire shelved wall display with them using modern art lights to spotlight each. The table is made from reclaimed Douglas fir with a skip-planed finish with three coats of clear water-based polyurethane. The whitewashed shiplap piece in the middle has been left in its original state and is from a 1910s dairy barn in Vancouver, Washington. The vintage Victorian bench is just one of the unique furniture pieces Salvage Works has in their showroom.

This beautiful guesthouse on the property of Jennifer's Gardens in Austin, Texas, is filled with reclaimed finds. In this stunning bathroom is a gorgeous door from Old World Antieks, in La Grange, Texas, an iron gate that is almost flush with the glass shower wall, and an antique pendant light from Round Top Antique Shows, in Round Top, Texas. These are just the larger salvage finds that make this bathroom so special. Jennifer and Fred took their time collecting all the elements, and the outcome was certainly worth the wait.

I love making vintage-inspired signs out of old reclaimed wood. When I saw this old door at the Country Living Fair in Atlanta, I knew it would make the perfect sign. After painting on the letters and adding a wax sealer, I used it as a piece of art in one of my design projects. If you want your sign to have a darker finish, you can use wax with a dark tint or even a poly that has a stain in it. Word art is so trendy, easy to make, and can be put anywhere in the house. No matter the room, you can add words like *bakery*, *love*, *bath*, *wash*, *groceries*, *dream*, or whatever word speaks to you and your family. I love doing sign workshops at fairs because I'm amazed at all the different looks, colors, and words that people use to reflect their own life and style. Some of the materials I use to make old signs are very wide reclaimed wood pieces, cabinet doors, and smaller doors that I find at salvage shops, rebuild centers, and antique fairs. Many times, these locations will have these old wood pieces in the back of the shop because they had a leftover door from a broken pine cupboard or something of the sort. All you have to do is ask if they have any old doors or cabinet pieces that you could buy, and then create your own sign.

4

The Celebration of Color

Ways to Get Creative with Color

Design today means mixing and matching a lot of color. Eclectic style uses colorful pillows, frames, bedding, tapestries, wood, furniture, and more. Often you'll find that lots of these furnishings, fixtures, and materials are secondhand. There are a number of different ways to work with color when using vintage and reclaimed materials. This chapter shows you how to get the look of today's trendiest shades, whether it's by repurposing pieces that already have color or adding color to old materials.

Interior designer Kim Deetjen and architectural designer Cliff Deetjen found this bright red metal antique piece at Anthony Catalfano Home, a home furnishing shop in Wells, Maine. But it was the story that caught their attention. The piece was once a Juliet balcony (a false balcony projecting from a wall of a building, usually in front of a window) from a ship captain's home on the southern coast of Maine. The balcony was turned upside down, sandblasted, and then sprayed with an automotive bright red lacquer paint. A piece of soapstone was then placed on top. This totally transformed piece now makes for a beautiful side table in the new entranceway off their kitchen. The red really pops off the shiplap white walls and the black stone floor, which in turn allows the character of the piece to stand out.

Here's a close-up look at a piece of wood and a bracket. The patina, layers, cracks, and wear give these pieces all the character they need. All you have to do is find a place to put them.

Taking Advantage of Patina

Vintage or antique furnishings, old doors, and pieces of wood often already have a layer of color on them. Some have worn-off paint that shows glimpses of the natural wood underneath, and some have so many layers of paint that it's like an Impressionist painting. Others are as bright as though they were painted yesterday. Each of these patinas tells a story, and instead of covering it up you can choose to enhance it. You can seal an existing paint job with a nontoxic wax, a polyurethane, an

The colors in this room work beautifully with the embroidered pillow. The vintage door headboard with muted paint was found at Old World Antieks, in La Grange, Texas. The red metal table is from Pottery Barn, and the antique lamp with an orange shade is from one of the many local Austin antique and vintage shops. Combined, these pieces give the guest room at Jennifer's Gardens, in Austin, Texas, a calming effect.

This original door at the Mad River Barn, in Vermont, had been set aside during the renovation project. But it was just one of the many pieces brought back to life as part of their renovation. Leaving the original patina intact (but sealing it well), the door is now a striking feature, and is one of the first things you see when you walk into the restaurant and pub. The textures and layers of red, white, and brown patinas all speak to the history of the old barn. Not only is this large door a functioning piece of the space, but it's the design focal point as well.

epoxy coat, or another finish (which is good to do if it's older paint, as paint from the mid 1970s or earlier may contain lead). Or you might choose to leave it unsealed if it was painted after the late 1970s. Letting the paint colors show gives you an opportunity to design and style around another piece with those same colors. Midcentury glass, for example, such as vases, goblets, and barware, are full of color. If you already have a color scheme going, then spend some time searching for pieces that would match or complement it. Whites, creams, and blues work well together, for example. Once you know what colors you're looking for, you will see them everywhere—in antique bowls, paintings, furniture, vintage textiles, and even reclaimed wood. So when shopping for pieces, look for ones that are in your color scheme and add them to your design.

It's fun to see the emergence of the adult coloring book craze. But crafters have known for centuries that working with your hands is relaxing. This beautiful crewel workpiece that I picked up at a secondhand shop took someone many, many hours to make. And though I wouldn't hang this in my home as is, I can still appreciate it in another way. By taking it out of the frame and finding some similar pieces, I was able to make some throw pillows. Now, I am surrounded by labors of love, but in a more modern bohemian way. When I visit secondhand shops, I can't help but pick up old crewel work and embroidery artwork pieces. Using some bedspreads my mom picked up for me at a garage sale for only a few dollars (they had holes in them) and adding these remarkable pieces of colorful textile art along with the vintage blankets that I've picked up all over the world, I've created this cozy spot that I never want to leave.

In her little purple cottage in Austin, Texas, Lucinda Hutson, a cookbook author and tequila expert, expresses her love for Mexican culture in many unique ways, including the set of stairs that leads to her backyard porches. Celia Berry, an Austin mosaic artist, used milagros (religious folk charms), other charms, broken tile, and ornaments to create this stairway that is bright, colorful, and fun. The result is a beautiful celebration of the Day of the Dead.

Creative Colorful Recycling

As a person who undertakes a lot of DIY projects, I have learned many ways to use color creatively. Cover scrap wood in colorful pieces of leftover fabrics, jeans, and dish towels. Add vintage plumbing handles in reds, blues, or yellows. Make a fruit basket out of colorful recycled wire. Opportunities to add color are everywhere—you just have to look around you and see what is already available to use. Some folks like colorful bottle caps; others like glass bottles, colorful frames, bright costume jewelry, antique books, pottery, dishware, glassware, knobs, lighting, or vintage rugs. All can be used for creative color recycling.

I made this modern, hip piece using stiff recycled wire I picked up at the scrap metal yard. Using my exercise ball as a base (it has to get used for something!), I taped some pieces down and then removed the ball. I then started wrapping other pieces around it, creating the bowl. This would also make great wall art.

It really doesn't take much to get kids involved in recycling and crafting. Here is a large vase I picked up at Goodwill. We had a bin of old duct tape left over from many years ago. When my daughter, Gabrielle, was a little kid, we just wrapped the tape around the vase. A simple, colorful project like this is a great way to get kids started with recycling and reusing.

Emily's master bathroom is a cornucopia of color. Many of the features were already in place when she and her husband bought the home, such as the vintage lighting, fixtures, and tub. They found the stained glass at the Round Top Antique Shows, in Round Top, Texas. During their travels they picked up the vintage pieces and collections that now sit on the antique dresser. The column in the room is decorative, and the incredible green patina door to the toilet area adds just a bit of privacy while letting light in. The whole room, with its hues of green, has an inviting spa-like feel with a Victorian flair.

Updating and Creating with Paint

One of the easiest ways to change up a space, a fixture, or a furnishing is by painting it. There are hundreds of paints out there, including chalk paints, milk paints, acrylics, and oils. You can create a high-gloss lacquer look, a whitewashed shabby-chic look, or even make a total transformation with patterns of stripes or circles—in any color.

Here are five things to consider before you whip out the paintbrush:

1. Is it an heirloom or antique piece? Will its value plummet if you paint it? If you're unsure, take a picture of it and ask a local antiques dealer for their opinion. You can also go online to check out sites that are selling similar items. Sometimes a piece just needs a good cleaning and polishing. And sometimes it should be left as is.

2. Do you have a good understanding of the current finish on the piece? It's all too easy to begin painting something only to discover it has a wax finish that is not always easy to paint over. There are tons of video tutorials online that can teach you painting techniques, including how to deal with different types of finishes, so watch a few before you pick up the brush. If you spot an item and love the way it's painted, ask the owner or seller how it was done. This will help you create the style, color, and finishes that you like.

3. Oil primer can be used with latex paint, but latex primer can't be used with oil paint. Staining a piece is permanent, but paint can usually be sanded and removed. These are some of the hard-and-fast rules to know, but it's always a good idea to talk to the staff at your local paint store about different types of paint before you make a purchase.

4. What is the style you're going for? How is the piece used? Answering these questions will help you determine the sheen of your finish. The types of finishes include flat, satin, semi-gloss, high-gloss, stained, tinted, whitewash, tinted wax, and more. Each type of finish will give your piece a different look.

Adding a shade of color to old wood can be fun. First, clean the wood. Then, using watered-down paint, put on a little, wait a bit, and then wipe some off. The depth of color you want will determine how much water you add to the paint and how long you leave it on before you wipe it down. If you want just a hint of color, then wipe it off immediately; if you want it to be almost totally saturated with color, leave it a while longer. You can always add more or sand it a bit to get the color patina just right. You can also really water down the paint to have it wipe off even faster. Use a scrap piece of wood to test your options. Using old reclaimed wood will automatically give you a variation in color due to unique oxidation and texture patterns. If you're looking for the even coat of a weathered look, then use a half-and-half mixture of water and paint and don't wipe any off.

5. Have you budgeted enough time? A quality paint job takes time and effort and a lot of prep work. Budget for this and you'll get a great finished product.

New Products Using Recycled Materials

Tiles, glass, countertops, recycled fabrics, and recycled carpets are just a few of the new products that have a ton of color in them. Bright greens, blues, yellows, reds—you name it, you can get it. FLOR carpet tile (sold

This old green table was found at the Country Living Fair in Nashville, the cherub lamp at another fair, and the cast-iron lion bookends at an antique shop. Combined with the DIY projects such as the paintbrush vase and recycled bicycle rim coated with scraps of ribbon, they together become a desk for a dreamer.

after

before

Anyone who knows me knows I'm all about comfort. Although this old brown chair I picked up at a recycling center is totally outdated (and the cushions were so gross I had to throw them away), I knew a couple of things about it. One: It was made from solid wood and was well built. Two: It was ridiculously comfortable. It was a shorter height, and the rocker worked well. I brought the chair home and livened it up with a fun paint job and some colorful new cushions. It's easy to change up some old furniture with paint. Here I did a freehand blue and white pattern, but you could do anything from dots to doves, zebra stripes, or chevron patterns.

Updating this townhouse half bath was as simple as freshening up the paint and installing a mural. To add a pop of color, I picked up an old barn wood mirror at Champlain Valley Antique Center, in Shelburne, Vermont. Many antique shops and rebuild centers not only sell vintage pieces but build their own pieces out of old wood, window frames, and other vintage materials they have. I also love to use gorgeous old pieces of trim I find at my local architectural salvage shop to create my own frames. They have a ton of character. And it's easy to make your own frame, using one of the many online tutorials. Once you've made a frame, bring it to your local glass shop and they'll cut a custom-sized mirror for you to put in it.

by several retailers and reps across the country and available online) is just one of many carpet products that use 100 percent recycled nylon, and they are well known for their vibrant colors and patterns.

Build a Color Palette around a Vintage Piece

There are times I'll start an entire design color palette around a small colorful bowl or a wooden box that has the perfect patina. If I already know the style of the space, then I usually know what colors I'm going to use. If I'm doing something industrial, I tend to go with blacks, reds, or browns. If a property is on the water, I'll often use blues, greens, and whites. For a modern feel, I stick with grays and whites with funky pops of bright colors. I'm all over the place! So if I see something that has the colors that I'm looking for, whether it's a quilt, a bright book jacket, or even a piece of artwork, I pick it up and start planning my color scheme around it.

How Old Becomes New

Here are just a few ideas for how some recycled materials can be made into new products.

RECYCLED ALUMINUM becomes cool modern metal chairs, side tables, cabinet hardware, sinks, and lighting.

RECYCLED GLASS becomes tile (any shape or size) for countertops, vanity tops, or aggregate in concrete counters or terrazzo-style flooring.

RECYCLED PLASTIC becomes area rugs, indoor and outdoor furniture, and even light fixtures.

RECYCLED PORCELAIN TOILETS AND SINKS become countertops and custom tile.

RECYCLED CARPETS become new carpets and carpet tiles.

Adding Color to Your Decor

It's not hard to work with color or to find it in salvaged furnishings and building materials. You have to be open to all possibilities. If you're just adding color to your decor, then your salvage and recycled possibilities are endless. To get started, create a list of your favorite colors. What colors do you want in your living room, bathroom, and bedroom? Don't be nervous about bold colors; just start small. Adding a bright picture frame, an old desk, a collection of bowls, or even a large old schoolroom lab jar filled with green plants are just a few ways to bring color into your decor. Collections are also fun ways to introduce color accents. Collect something as simple as classic tinted mason jars. Once you've gathered a few items, work on how to style them, such as in a wall display, stacked along a back wall, spread across a large table, or even on a mantel.

Top, left to right: Like the Island of Misfit Toys, the colorful textiles in this glorious pile are waiting for just the right piece of furniture that will show off their character and bring them back to life. Leland Duck, of the upholstery company Revive Upholstery & Design, in Portland, Oregon, picks these materials up on his travels. From duffel bags to tent covers, from rugs to quilts, each piece of textile tells a story, one that will carry on through the finished reupholstered pieces.

This flower vase was so easy to make. It would be a great project to do with kids or even adults who are new to the whole DIY world. I grabbed a recycled jar (a jam one will do) and placed a rubber band around it. I slid leftover craft paintbrushes under the rubber band, and once I had them all in, I wrapped twine around the jar to hide the rubber band. Voilà! An instant flower vase in less than 10 minutes. You can use a smaller recycled jar and old nails or a larger jar and larger paintbrushes or vintage screwdrivers or even painted sticks. The possibilities are endless.

Bottom, left to right: When people think of recycled or vintage materials, they usually tend to think big. But even the smallest things can be reused. I picked up the bicycle rim at my local metal scrap yard, the yarn at Goodwill, the scraps of fabric (that I ripped into ribbons) at another secondhand shop, and the doilies at a church shop (only open for a few hours a week). From all this I created a fun red, white, and blue dream catcher, which is great for cottage wall art or a fun patriotic party. There are so many simple ways to bring color into your space. Have fun with color, and dream on.

I love vintage rugs, but often I find them too fragile or too historic to actually put down on the floor to be walked on. I find that old rugs make great wall art (and help with sound issues). Here at the pub entrance at Mad River Barn, in Waitsfield, Vermont, I created wall art out of a Native American rug I found at Champlain Valley Antique Center, in Shelburne, Vermont. I hung it from old wood and piping that came out of the renovation project itself. I just added some hardware curtain rings to keep it in place. This handmade textile art is a piece of history on display.

I love shopping at my local antique shops, such as Champlain Valley Antique Center in Vermont. Wandering through the aisles looking at colors and pieces inspires me for my next design project. For example, this pink chair would be dazzling in a bright-white modern powder room as a vanity chair, or just precious in a little girl's room that is filled with hues of pink and cream. What do you see in this picture that inspires color ideas for you?

Pops of Color

Many times when I'm designing I use neutral colors as my backdrop on walls, ceilings, and wainscoting. This allows me to add color in ways that are more easily changeable, such as art, pillows, bedding, and furniture. Sometimes it only takes one stand-out piece to transform a room. It can be a wall of framed pictures of colorful birds (pulled from an old book), or a huge sign painted in red and white. It can be a wild crochet bedspread thrown on the end

Accepting Imperfection

THE JAPANESE SAYING *WABI-SABI* ENCAPSULATES THE ACCEPTANCE OF TRANSIENCE AND OF IMPERFECTION IN THE AESTHETIC OF YOUR HOME. Many reclaimed, recycled, and vintage materials have natural imperfections, acquired through the passage of time. Let's embrace these individual flaws as part of the history and character of these materials. Let go of the idea of perfection and celebrate unique character instead. By renouncing the idea of perfection we can create homes that are welcoming, comfortable, and most important, our own.

Kim and Cliff Deetjen's contemporary addition to their home has a bright and cheery color scheme that is emphasized with some gorgeous pieces, including this Northern European hand-painted rocking chair they found at an antique shop. The muted color tones in the chair are made even more noticeable by the vividly striped stair runner that showcases the same hues.

Above: This Tiffany-style lamp has been in Emily's home for many years. She saw it during an auction and fell in love with its colors, style, and sense of romance. She has since taken it from home to home. Here it sits on a garage sale find, a green metal outdoor table, against a reclaimed-wood wall painted in hues of green and blue. This is a great example of how tones of similar colors, such as these various shades of blue-greens, can enhance and highlight each other.

Above: Shannon Quimby, a designer and stylist in Portland, Oregon, used new tiles made from recycled materials in her son's bathroom. Bright blues and whites in a subway pattern line the shower while the recycled tiles transition to only white on the countertop and shower floor. The shape and color of the tile, the dark grout, and layout pattern give this bathroom a vintage look with a modern flair. The vintage beam is painted in a high-gloss white and makes for a very unique threshold for the shower space.

of a bed, a vintage textile piece used as curtains, a coffee table painted with the Union Jack, or a recycled dresser given a coat of purple paint and polka dots for a kid's room. These are easy additions without making structural changes or big design alterations.

Kim Clements and Joe Schneider, owners of the Seattle design/building firm, JAS Design Build, have a casual, comfortable look in their own renovated home. Their living room is an eclectic showcase for their unique finds, such as the colorful 1930s Iranian rug, the chair Kim found at a garage sale and she reupholstered, a vintage blue wool blanket and pillow, and the antique tea table that holds just a few of their books. The combination makes for a happy, welcoming spot.

Find your tribe.
Love them hard.

skuut

Paige and her family (including five dogs and a few birds) have a fun house in Vermont. Open and welcoming to all, Paige loves incorporating her finds throughout the house, including the blue bench that was once the end of a bunk bed bought at a garage sale. The red-seated stools were picked up at a university warehouse sale, the old wood is from a friend's barn, and the many, many bottle caps were collected by her son, friends, and family to create this entertaining floor for the bar area. Paige believes that designing and decorating with recycled goods is all about embracing your passions and finding others who feel the same way.

Above, left: This display of recycled bottle caps at Paige's home is an example of the daily happiness in reusing old materials. In listening to Paige tell the story of all the recycled items in her home, including how friends and family gathered bottle caps, and how her son brought her back bottle caps from around the world to help create the floor, you couldn't help but smile and feel her joy. Does it make you happy? If so, then by all means reclaim it.

Above, right: As the new designer for Basin Harbor, a historic lakefront resort in Vermont, I'm slowly going through each of their 74 cottages, lodge rooms, and public spaces to give them new life, many times with old things. I'm scouring the numerous attics on the 700-acre property to search for the family's own heirloom pieces, and I'm bringing them back into the rooms so that guests can get a sense of the history of the resort and the five generations of family who have lived and worked there. In this cottage, most of the nightstands and pieces of the outdated orangey pine furniture were painted a bright blue. The walls were stripped of their old wallpaper and painted a calming neutral color so the cool vintage accents could stand out, such as these old bright orange life buoys that flank the bed.

My friend Beverly Martinets and I worked on a DIY project together at her bed and breakfast, Bel Solé, in Carmine, Texas. Using pieces of wallpaper, we created a whole new look for the stairway that goes to her upstairs guest rooms. This type of colorful upcycled project is fun to do with friends and only takes a couple of days (allowing for drying time). You can use vintage muted color paper like we did here for a warm and romantic style, or go wild and use bold vintage papers to change things up.

How to Upcycle Stair Risers with Vintage Wallpaper

1. Sand and clean stairs.
2. Tape around edges and risers.
3. Cut vintage wallpaper to size.
4. Decoupage both sides onto riser, getting out air bubbles.
5. Let dry.
6. Add gold paint stencils.
7. Let dry.
8. Seal with polyurethane, two to three coats.
9. Go around edges of wallpaper with clear caulking.
10. Remove tape.

The main living space in Jennifer and Fred's guest cottage is filled with colorful finds. The vintage Mexican table with its orange hues and the bright chairs found in New Mexico are complemented by the vintage blue bottles on the table and the Native American carvings on the wall. The front doors are vintage French doors that they found in San Antonio, Texas. The doors sat in storage for 10 years until Jennifer and Fred were ready to use them for this project. The brick floor is made from reclaimed Chicago brick they picked up by the pallet at a reclaimed materials warehouse store. As you look at all the pieces and materials used in this space, notice how all these bold statements work well together, none outshining another. The beautiful muted backdrops (walls, doors, and flooring) allow the colorful pieces to stand out.

At the Junk Gypsy store, in Round Top, Texas, you'll see lots of examples of furniture painted brightly with their very own line of paint: from dressers to wood walls to metal lampshade frames. If you love the way a piece is painted, ask them how they did it. The items in this store may help you get an idea of the style, color, and finishes that you like. Here, the vintage dresser with mirror was painted with the color Buttermilk Biscuit, and then slightly sanded to bring out a bit of the original wood color underneath. The shorter side table tucked under the dresser was painted with the color Gypsy Prom and finished with a low-sheen wax. The metal lampshade is wrapped in pink velvet ribbon, which is a great way to update old shades. The wood walls were given a whitewash finish.

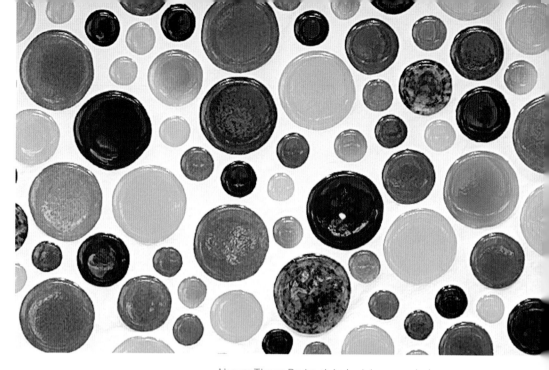

Above: These Bedrock Industries recycled glass circle tiles are natural colors that come from items such as old bottles, streetlamps, and vintage windows. Crushed, melted down, and turned into tile, they make for a fun, colorful backsplash or shower wall. Using all one color, such as the sea glass green or a blue, with a smaller grout width, you can easily have a sophisticated palette while still embracing color. Recycled glass comes in an abundance of colors and sizes to fit your design needs. Glass is a great material for bathrooms because it's not porous and does not absorb moisture, plus it is pretty easy to clean.

Left: These bottles have been cleverly put together to create useful rain gutters. Created by Bedrock Industries, in Seattle, from recycled bottles, they show us that recycling is not only fun but functional. These sculptural works of art add color to any home. Bedrock Industries focuses on the needs of conscious consumers, and they have recycled thousands of tons of glass into tiles, home decor, aggregate for concrete and countertops, and much more. Their company, which creates gorgeous glass tiles that are 100 percent recycled with no unnatural dyes added, is just one of many around the nation that can help you design and decorate your home with products that you'll feel great about.

One of the focal points in Emily's rental cabin in Texas is the bathroom door. This antique door with its stained glass window not only adds character and color to this small cabin, but allows light to penetrate into the bathroom while maintaining privacy. The wainscoting on the wall is painted in a washed blue-green. Colorful stained glass doors can usually be found at architectural salvage shops. These types of antique doors help brighten up a dark hallway or a bathroom that doesn't have a window. Have fun with these statement pieces by using them in your bathrooms, entranceways, walk-in closets, and pantries.

I picked up this robin egg blue table at The Vintage Bazaar, in Salisbury, Massachusetts. I loved the color and the wear on it, and I didn't do a thing except seal it with a coat of wax. The boxes behind the desk are old wooden video storage boxes I picked up for a few dollars each from my neighbor Mike. (It's good to be known as the salvage girl on the street.) Using a package of floral napkins and some decoupage glue, I created some colorful fronts on the boxes, making them ideal for office storage containers while adding color and style to the room. I picked up the throw at a vintage fair. With just a few pieces, I fashioned a bright and cheery office/study area, which would work perfectly for a tiny house or small apartment.

after

before

before

This outdated living room was turned around with some budget-friendly fixes, including some new and vintage furnishings, and a wall display of baskets painted in grays, blacks, and whites. Baskets are a very affordable way to add simple decor to any room. Paint them all shades of pink for a kid's bedroom or all shades of black for a modern industrial loft.

after

I was on the hunt for wood to use on a dining room wall when, at the rebuild center in central Vermont, I came across a pile of blue paneling. It was way in the back, almost behind the building, wet and in disarray, but that didn't deter me. As I went through the pile (discarding pieces that were too rotten to use), I tried to determine if I actually would have enough to create a distinctive wall for a bedroom on the same project. Taking a chance, I bought it all for a mere $25 (the paneling was cheap because it needed a ton of work). We let the wood dry completely, and then we followed the lead paint guidelines for restoration, just in case the pieces were painted before 1978. We added the pieces to the bedroom wall and sealed it well. We moved out the existing bedroom set, and using some gorgeous reclaimed wood we created new side tables and a headboard.

before

5

Black, White, and Natural Colors

The Power of Keeping It Simple, Monochromatic, and Natural

Designs using all black, white, cream, and natural wood colors can be glamorous, romantic, shabby chic, and even modern, depending on what materials are used and how they are put together. This chapter highlights some interesting ways to create one-of-a-kind items using some seriously easy design ideas.

This gorgeous custom-made table was built with reclaimed materials from a 1700s barn in central Vermont that was deconstructed by Mason Brothers Architectural Salvage Warehouse. After picking out the wood, my friend Bret and I strapped it to his truck and brought it to his garage, where he created this amazing table. Notice how the gorgeous coat of gray stain allows for the original color and character of the wood to shine through. This piece is filled with history and fits perfectly in this contemporary lakefront home. Reclaimed wood doesn't need to look old, rustic, or country.

Need a great gift idea? Simply pick up some reclaimed wood and craft your very own modern black-and-white coasters. Using painter's tape, outline the edge of the wood, and then paint the middle white. Apply a couple of coats. Once the paint is dry, add your design. Think stripes, circles, rings, chevron pattern, checkered . . . I've even painted these with sports team logos. You will probably need two coats of black paint for the design. Add some felt pads and a black-and-white ribbon, and you'll be the hit of any holiday or birthday party.

50 Shades of Black and White

There are cool colors, warm colors, and neutral colors. There are yellow tones, gray tones, red tones, blue tones . . . so many that it gets a little crazy. There are hundreds of shades of colors, and when you're in a paint store looking at chips it can be a little overwhelming. But if you have a feel for shade and tone options, it will be easier to decide what you want in your home. If you're not sure about cool colors or warm colors, or about a blue versus red undertone, just head into your local paint shop and get a little education. They will be happy to help.

Painting

One of the easiest ways to change reclaimed and recycled furnishings and materials to a monochrome look is with paint. The great thing about paint is that it can really pull pieces together, no matter how different

My friends at The Wall Doctor, a wallpaper and blinds store, in Burlington, Vermont, held on to their old wallpaper books for me. I used the pages to create a new look for a wall, giving it a bold and exciting black-and-white style. If you have a small space, or just need a change, something as simple as poster putty and recycled wallpaper or dictionary pages will do.

after

before

before

I have a tiny guest bedroom that has absolutely no storage. So when I found this old cedar chest at the ReSource Building Material Store, in Burlington, Vermont for $100, I knew I had to get it. It was a quality piece, with dovetail joints and fully lined with cedar inside. And although it was a nice piece, it was not a valuable antique. The laminate top was chipped a little and the front was scratched up, but I knew I was going to give it a fun paint job so that didn't worry me. I sanded the piece well (not my favorite part), and then gave it a coat of black paint with a matte finish, and then another one. Once that was dry, slowly, over the course of a few days, I hand painted on shapes and patterns, letting each area dry before moving on to the next. I used stencils as well as hand painted areas. Once I was done painting the designs, I gave the whole piece a wax finish. Now, with my bone inlay-inspired painted chest, I can store my bulky sweaters while giving my guests a little space for their stuff.

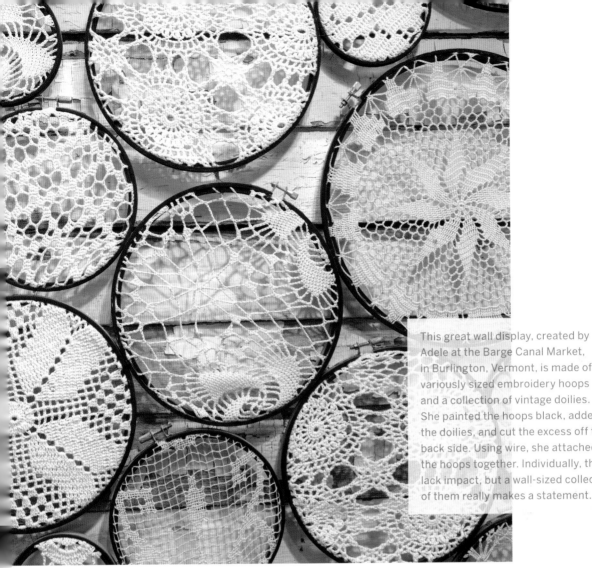

This great wall display, created by Adele at the Barge Canal Market, in Burlington, Vermont, is made of variously sized embroidery hoops and a collection of vintage doilies. She painted the hoops black, added the doilies, and cut the excess off the back side. Using wire, she attached the hoops together. Individually, they lack impact, but a wall-sized collection of them really makes a statement.

they are in style, shape, or structure. For example, picture an entire wall of frames of all different shapes and sizes. A black matte finish with a wax coat for the frames creates a modern look. Now imagine those frames in a glossy white for a gorgeous, high-end look. Try whitewash instead for a shabby-chic look. Note that there are numerous techniques for whitewashing, so do a little research on the exact look you want and which technique you should use.

It's amazing how something can be totally transformed with the right finish and gloss. If you can, test some sample colors before you try one on your piece. Also, really understand the current finish on the reclaimed material. If it already has a lacquer on it, then that finish will need to be completely sanded off before you

Above, left: Finding reclaimed wood with character is as simple as walking into your salvage yard. What's a little more difficult is trying to figure out the style and color of your project. Working with older wood can be a little more complicated, so try to work with the salvage yard on picking out the pieces that are the straightest and have the least amount of cracks. Also make sure that none of the wood you bring home has any soft or rotted areas. This wood is beautiful as is, and we used it in a variety of projects, including a custom modern bathroom vanity and the beautiful gray stained table in this contemporary lakefront home. It would also make an amazing rustic-style farmhouse table with a wax finish. If you're using wood this old, let the character speak for itself, because it's all the design you'll need.

Above, right: The warm wood, clean lines, and bold statements create a stunning entranceway bathroom in this lakefront home. The antique mirror was found at a flea market in Europe. The vanity was custom made with the reclaimed wood and a custom marble sink. The large apron on the front of the vanity shows the character of the wood that was taken from an 18th-century barn, and it hides all the plumbing. The juxtaposition of the elegant antique gold-framed mirror and the rustic wood blends perfectly with the rest of the space.

Below: Another gorgeous touch in Paige and Smoot's home is the beautiful bench in the master bedroom. This reclaimed wood bench, which was picked up at Old World Antieks, in La Grange, Texas, works beautifully with the natural palette of the bedding and rug. The vintage leather bag was found at a secondhand shop. A bench at the end of a bed is also a nice touch in a guest bedroom or vacation rental property, because it's always helpful for guests to be able to drop their suitcase on it for easy access.

Above, left: Paige and Smoot Hull's new linen closet in their addition at The Vintage Round Top, in Round Top, Texas, is made with vintage shutters they fell in love with in an antique store in New Orleans. They sealed the chipping paint and left the patina as is. These doors make an ordinary linen closet feel like a piece of art.

apply anything new. If the wood is very dry, it will soak in the paint so quickly that you'll need multiple layers and a fantastic primer.

When you're out shopping don't walk past a piece that doesn't fit your color scheme or style. Chances are you can paint it to fit your needs. I usually find quality, paintable pieces at used furniture shops or recycle centers. As for finds at antique shops, I'm more likely to leave those items in their original finish and just give them a good cleaning.

after

This renovated bedroom at the Mad River Barn is an ideal example of how to use a natural wood barn door to shape a space. This once oversized room had two double beds in it. It now has a queen bed area as well as built-in bunk beds, separated by a reclaimed wood sliding door. The door was built from the antique wood that came out of the barn during the renovation. The wood was cleaned up, sanded, and sealed, and then put together with cross wood to create the door. This type of construction, vertical wood with two horizontal pieces, is a very simple way to build a vintage-inspired sliding barn door. The slider brackets came from the hardware store and were sprayed black. The bed frame was made from old beams that have 2" × 4"s cross-cut into them. They were painted black too. The rest of the space has warm woods, metals, and neutral colors to create a modern farmhouse feel with an industrial edge.

before

Wendy Lewis, owner of The Textile Trunk, an online store, lives in a Greek revival farmhouse built in 1912. Originally a large home, she turned it into a duplex. The space that was once the library is now her kitchen. Wendy took advantage of the shelving and cabinetry that was already in place, and then added a vintage enamel cast-iron sink purchased at Mason Brothers Architectural Salvage Warehouse; her collection of modern, vintage, and antique French and American pottery; as well as English ironstone dating from the 18th century to today, all in a white and cream palette. She sanded down and whitewashed the original floors, giving this room the feel of a French country home.

Designing

Sometimes you don't want to paint anything yourself or do any work, you just want cool vintage or recycled pieces in black, white, or natural colors. That's simple enough to do. Materials and furnishings that are already in those colors can be found at a variety of places. For example, if I'm looking for wood to plank walls or to build tables or to make signs, I look for painted wood in those colors at my local rebuild center or salvage shop. If I'm trying to create a backsplash or tabletop with salvaged or scrap pieces of stone or tile, such as marble, granite, soapstone, or slate, I head to my stone masonry shop. They usually have backyards (stone graveyards) with tons of scrap, leftover pieces, end cuts, and more at reasonable rates. I'm a huge fan of vintage white cast-iron enamel sinks, and I use them in my designs whenever I can. They can be found at salvage shops or online.

Repurposed furniture in white, black, or natural colors can be found at vintage fairs and shops that are known for upcycling furniture. Two such examples are Vintage Inspired Lifestyle Marketplace, in Burlington,

New York City designer Kelly Giesen is in love with salvage finds. This high-end apartment is filled with them. The old doors that lead to the bathroom now have a coat of crisp white paint. The original glass pieces were taken out and mirrors installed. This creates privacy in the bathroom and makes the apartment look bigger and brighter with the reflection into the room. The upper cabinet doors in the kitchen and all the rest of the doors in the apartment are also vintage salvaged pieces, mostly from Olde Good Things. The vintage midcentury light fixture was found in an antique shop, and most of the glassware and canisters in the kitchen are also antique and vintage pieces that have been collected over the years. This apartment showcases old pieces that are full of detail and character, but the overall effect creates a look that is glamorous and new. The high-gloss paint makes this space look crisp, modern, and clean while allowing for the details of the old pieces to stand out.

The bedrooms at Mad River Barn are kept pretty simple. The renovation included painting the outdated orange-tinted pine paneling a creamy white and having the old wool blankets cleaned. My daughter and I made decorative pillows out of them, using fabric paint, letter stencils, and black embroidery thread. As for the wall art, I created some very simple pieces using scraps of lumber that I pulled out of the garbage during the construction process. These little pieces had no value for the construction team, but I loved the natural and painted creamy patinas of the boards. I took some of my own photography and had them printed out in black and white. Using small upholstery nails, I attached them to the scraps of wood.

Vermont, and Junk Gypsy, in Round Top, Texas. Look for shops in your area that refinish furniture with paint. I find my vintage textiles at fairs such as the Brimfield Antique Show, Country Living Fairs, garage sales, online textile companies, and my local secondhand shops, like Goodwill, Habitat for Humanity, and The Salvation Army.

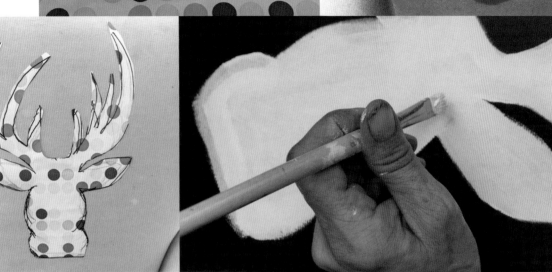

My neighbor gave me an old cream-colored chair she was no longer using. It had a few stains on it but the quality of the chair was excellent. Using Simply Spray, an upholstery spray paint, I created a fun contemporary look for my "new" chair. Using sticky-backed drawer liner, I cut out the shape of a deer head (found online). Then I stuck it to the back of the chair and sprayed the upholstery paint around the design, making sure to have a rag handy to clean up the drips. After a few coats (drying in between), I had a charcoal-colored chair. I peeled off the sticker, and then using craft fabric paint in white I painted the deer head shape.

Small Touches, Displaying, and Collecting

A scrap of wood, a white board for making a sign, layers of chenille bedspreads, an entire wall of ironstone platters: Small touches like these are easy ways to bring white, black, or natural colors into your rooms. For example, old wool blankets are often too stained or, frankly, too itchy to use on your bed as a coverlet or blanket. But you can wash them on high heat to soften them up and give them a boiled wool look and feel. If these blankets have a stain or two, you can cut them into pillows, curtains, or even a bed skirt. If the blanket has a beautiful design on it, use it as wall art. If it

Opposite page: The new soaking tub in one of Bev Martinets' bed and breakfast guest bathrooms sits proudly in front of the gorgeous south-facing windows, which are flanked by vintage white bed sheets that have been turned into curtains. The lace gives the bather privacy, while the natural wood stool (picked up at Flown the Coop antique shop), which Bev had her builder friend add shelving to, is just the thing for towels, soap, and candles. Simple, yet functional, this white and neutral bathroom is relaxing and spa-like.

Left: In a window seat at Bev's house, layers of white make a cozy nook. The vintage curtains were saved from a deteriorating box of linens found in a friend's barn. Most of them were ruined, but she made tiebacks from the material she was able to save. She found the old door-turned-mirror at the Round Top Antique Show, and the vintage white and cream pillows and blankets have been collected over the years. The orange vase and teacup and saucer (saved from a fire) once belonged to her grandmother. This great example of layering shows how you can give a blank slate a sense of depth and character by using vintage pieces.

doesn't have a design, you can add your own with upholstery or fabric paint. Using a stencil, you can add flowers, or using painter's tape, you can make stripes and block lettering for a more modern look. Blankets are just the starting point for creative design work. For example, an old off-white rug can be turned into a black-and-white striped piece of art using upholstery spray paint.

Another way to approach small touches for these colors would be a coffee mug display. You can pick up a variety of white mugs from Goodwill, garage sales, or similarly affordable secondhand spots. Or you could build a simple shelving system with reclaimed wood and brackets and collect white bowls. Not only will they look gorgeous on display, but you can grab one when you need

Above: This is a close-up picture of an item that inspires me for future design work. It gives me ideas for design, patterns, and colors, perhaps in a modern Western home. I'm waiting for the perfect project, but until then I'll keep this picture in my inspiration file. When you see colors that inspire you, take a picture. You think you'll remember the look, tone, or patina—but chances are you won't. I can also tell you that without a picture it's hard to describe these one-of-a-kind looks, colors, and tones to other people.

Left: Bev Martinets purchased this vintage dresser at McCall Style, in Carmine, Texas. She removed the back piece before adding a skirt and feet on the bottom to bring the old dresser up to vanity height. She purchased the new vessel sink and faucet at her local hardware store and transformed this low vintage white dresser into a gorgeous bathroom vanity for her guest room. It is surprisingly easy to raise a low dresser that you love up to the proper height for kitchen islands, bathroom vanities, and bedside tables using blocking and trim, screw-in bun feet, table legs from the hardware store, or even cart wheels from a tractor supply company.

after

In the Jack and Jill bathroom of Gideon's townhouse redo, I reused the cabinet that was already there, but had it painted a light gray. We removed the top, added some reclaimed vintage wood, and placed the drop-in cast-iron sinks I had picked up at ReSource Building Material Store, in Burlington, Vermont. I found the tile online—left over from someone else's project—and had just enough for the back wall, which really transformed the space and gave it its wow appeal. The reclaimed wood adds warmth to the space while the new materials give a clean, fresh look, allowing for modern amenities. All the pieces that were removed from the bathroom were donated to a local rebuild center, which came and picked everything up. Some rebuild centers will not only pick up old items but will deconstruct them for you as well.

before

Old, enamel, cast-iron, double-drainboard sinks are making a comeback. They are not only functional, but they make a great statement piece in any kitchen. This sink, in Bev Martinets' Bel Solé bed and breakfast in Carmine, Texas, is a great example of how a statement piece can be the focal point of a design. Bev takes full advantage of the sink's large capacity and design. These sinks can be found at architectural salvage shops and online. Make sure to take into consideration the depth of the sinks and the width of the drainboards when building cabinetry around them.

it for mixing or putting out dinner. Another budget-friendly way of adding a small decorative touch is to find old frames and paint them in black and white, then layer them on a wall. This is especially fun if your wall is painted a bright cheery color. Or how about a collection of white vases sitting on a white wood fireplace mantel, filled with white roses or side-of-the-road Queen Anne's lace? The result is a lovely French country or shabby-chic look.

These are just a few examples of the thousands of ways you can give your room a monochromatic, modern, clean, country, or natural look.

Temporary Solutions

Sometimes you just want to change things up but you don't want to make the changes permanent or spend a fortune. You can achieve temporary changes in a variety of ways with very little cost. You could cover an entire wall with curtains or even

The other half of Wendy Lewis's old library room is now her dining area. This French country look started with a custom-made table by Champlain Valley Antique Center from old Vermont flooring. Then she reupholstered the antique French chairs in her own grain sack fabrics that she sells online. The cabinet she picked up at an antique shop, and the curtains are from the 1700s. The hand-stitched pieces were once hand and foot towels (yes, foot towels were a thing back then). All she did to create these lovely romantic curtains was add the antique metal rings and put them on a spring rod in the window. A friend found the door and door frame (originally painted orange) for her at a salvage yard in upstate New York. Her flooring was given a whitewash. Put all these white, cream, and whitewashed pieces together, and you have a dreamy French country look.

The printed fabric on this upholstered chair is an old German grain sack. Slip covering a more modern chair with vintage linens, grain sacks, or cream-colored bedding is an easy way to bring a shabby-chic or French country look into your dining room.

Left: In Wendy Lewis's old home, this room was originally used for sick family members. No longer in need of a "sick room," Wendy transformed this space into a spa-like bathroom. The sink was from a salvage shop in Rhode Island. She added vintage wide pine floors, and made the mirror out of the same pine. The wall sconce she found at the Brimfield Antique Show. The textile is a blue and white ikat, French flamme fabric from the 1750s–1760s. It is handwoven, a truly difficult piece to make, and something you don't see in today's textiles. The vintage 19th-century French tiebacks add a little flair. The metal janitor bucket, used as a trash can, was picked up in England. Traveling in the search for textiles for her company, Wendy has found some unique pieces for her own home.

Right: Designer Jessica Helgerson and her husband, architect Yianni Doulis, used reclaimed wood in their tiny 540-square-foot Oregon home. The wood used in all the walls, shelving, and built-ins originally came from a building that was once a house for shipyard workers in the 1940s, before it floated downstream in a flood and became a goose-checking station (where hunters would check in their geese). After all the wood was cleaned and sanded, they tied it together with a flat-finish white paint. The shiplap pattern gives the room a modern farmhouse feel and the built-in couch, with cotton charcoal-colored fabric, works perfectly with the filled bookshelves, making you want to sit down and read all day.

Kim and Mark Gaynor truly live the vintage lifestyle. Their company, Living Vintage, deconstructs old houses and builds and renovates with reclaimed materials. Their 1853 historic dogtrot house, in Alto, Texas, is filled with unique vintage finds and design touches. Dogtrot homes, also known as breezeway homes, are called this because of their central open breezeway area that connects two enclosed halves of a house by a roof. They were popular in the 19th and early 20th centuries, and were built to encourage airflow. These homes, unique to the South, are now being enclosed and updated while keeping their history alive. Kim and Mark's bedroom is filled with whites, creams, and natural colors. The original wood floor had a dark stain from the previous owners, but they were able to sand it down and refinish it beautifully. They built their own bed frame out of reclaimed porch posts and brackets. A vintage door serves as a headboard and an old ceiling tin is the footboard. They added a tin ceiling, painted it white, and updated an old brown dresser with a painted white shabby-chic look. Using old dressers as their nightstands helped balance the large bed and expansive space. Other touches, such as the vintage stained glass piece Kim's sister gave her and the antique floor lamps and artwork, make this an appealing room.

Sometimes it's as easy as finding a new purpose for a vintage piece. I purchased this old plant stand from Matthew Mead, a fellow stylist, at a vintage fair. Here I'm using it for a photo shoot with Gardener's Supply Company, in Burlington, Vermont, to show off their gorgeous holiday lights. With a vintage white tablecloth, some glass- and gold-antique plates, and a little greenery, this old three-tiered stand-turned-dessert-tray is ready for an elegant holiday party. You'll likely see these stands in stores in their original dark brown wood, but that's easily changed with a coat of paint.

sheets, giving the space texture and character—think a vintage painter's tarp with a huge black painting or word art. Other quick fixes include throwing some old bedspreads over a chair or a couch, or layering a wall with overlapping black frames that contain pictures from old books (think bird books, dictionaries with pictures, or old-school anatomy books). Sometimes you just need a change, and using affordable reclaimed materials can help you try things out and play with your space.

This display is so simple. I covered an extra-large glass vase I found at Goodwill with cream-colored scarves that friends had made me or that I had bought secondhand. In just a few minutes, I created a winter wonderland display on my entryway table. The table is a vintage Stickley, a gorgeous and valuable piece I bought at an antique shop and would never repurpose. The mirror, a gift from my friend Shannon Quimby, was made with vintage white trim. It was picked up at Mason Brothers Architectural Salvage Warehouse, in Essex Junction, Vermont. The old suitcase is from Vintage Inspired Lifestyle Marketplace, in Burlington, Vermont. The moment I walk in the door to my home, I'm happy, because I'm surrounded by unique treasures and gifts that have meaning to me and my family, with lovely stories behind them.

While walking through Five Corners Antiques, in Essex Junction, Vermont, I came across this basket of vintage sterling silver bowls and platters. Curious, I reached for the price tag attached to the basket. It was $14 for the whole lot. Could that be right? Now, frankly, I didn't really need an entire basket of old silver bowls, but a deal like that was too good to pass up. So like Red Riding Hood, I walked out the door with a basket in my hands, proving that sometimes you just have to go with the flow. With my finds, I created a beautiful display above my 1880s soapstone laundry sink. I placed recycled plastic containers inside them (think yogurt cups), and then filled them with dirt, moss, foliage, plants, and succulents. For the holidays, I dress them up with red berries and silver leaves. The soapstone countertop is made from 24" × 24" pieces of soapstone tile, and the backsplash is made from pieces my husband and I found in the scrap pile at the stone yard. He cut them all with a tile saw, and we installed our own countertop over a weekend. My husband made the coffeemaker, using old school lab pieces, and gave it to me as a Christmas gift. It's fun to make coffee in it every morning.

Salvage expert and homeowner Shannon Quimby shows us how to bring old and new together in a modern way in this mudroom entranceway. There once stood a cottage on the same land, and all the materials that could be salvaged from it were reused in the new home. This included the old siding wood that now serves as the unique wall paneling, as well as the old electrical knobs that are now used as cabinet hardware. The flooring, once an old bowling alley lane, adds some character and whimsy. By using eco paint and other environmentally friendly materials, plus eschewing a dumpster and recycling everything in the course of the renovation, Shannon set a high mark for reusing, recycling, and using eco-friendly building standards in her home renovation.

after

before

I was thrilled when June and Wendell Anderson asked me to help redesign some of the spaces in the old Bundy Center for the Arts, in Waitsfield, Vermont (built in 1962 by Harlow Carpenter). Today it's both their home and a center for arts and events, called The Bundy Modern. This old storage space is now their bright and beautiful kitchen. In keeping with the building's architecture and modern design, we renovated using new materials as well as some old ones. The antique corner cabinet, found at Mason Brothers Architectural Salvage Warehouse, was painted a bright white to blend in with the modern tile. The table in the middle was made from the wall that was cut out to create an opening between the kitchen and the dining area. The black and white theme, mixing old and new, works well throughout the rooms in this midcentury modern building.

6

Big Impacts, Little Touches, and Cool Collections

Enjoying, Styling, and Displaying Your Treasures

Sometimes it just takes that one thing, like a large vintage trunk, or a variety of small things put together, such as an entire wall of printer block words, to create a BIG impact. We should never discount the importance of what we collect, and how we display it. Whether it's the small touches that bring us great pleasure and kindle fond memories on a daily basis or the big statement pieces that really transform our spaces, these should both be given equal weight. This chapter will show rooms that create a wow factor through

In a single afternoon, interior and jewelry designer Renee Tornabene created her own wall shelving unit with an old window, some chalk paint, hardware store wood, and brackets. This instant shelving unit for everyday use in her quaint Arizona townhouse is where she displays her vintage kitchen pieces and antique bowls and finds. This is a great idea for tiny homes, apartments, and small kitchens, because it adds character and functionality at the same time. Old windows can be found at rebuild centers, secondhand shops, and architectural salvage centers, or even on the side of the road. Single-pane windows can no longer be used when homes are remodeled to bring them up to code, but it doesn't mean we can't use them in our decor. Use them to create fun items such as this shelving unit, mirrors, chalkboard message boards, jewelry holders, and much more.

Because June and Wendell Anderson's home was once an art and sculpture gallery, it has some pretty unique living spaces, such as large gallery rooms, loft areas, and very high ceilings. To redo the loft area, which serves as their living room, we didn't change much at all. We painted the walls and rearranged the furniture they had brought from their old home. Nina, the dog, loves the expansive new space. With large walls like these you can get creative with your artwork. I created these pieces of feather artwork over a few long, cold, winter nights at home while I watched TV. I cut some recycled paper bags from the grocery store into pieces, then I laid them out in a collage fashion and taped them together with duct tape. After the paper was put back together, I took a pencil and drew some feathers. Once that was done, and I felt good about the shapes and sizes, I used some black paint and an artist's paintbrush to follow the pencil marks and create the drawings (then I erased any pencil marks I could still see). This may be one of the least expensive ways to make large pieces of wall art. The midcentury-inspired furniture, vintage table, and lamp work great with the funky art pieces.

one piece, a collection of items, or distinctive design ideas. As you will see, there are large and tiny ways to bring joy into your home's design and decor with little effort.

Large Pieces That Make Big Impacts

Sometimes it takes only one thing to change an entire room: an extra-large vintage sign, a huge coffee table made from an old barn door, a chest of drawers the size of a small

Kim and Mark Gaynor know how to collect. Once the breezeway area of their dogtrot house (now enclosed), this area serves as a fabulous place for them to show off their book collections and to have large family gatherings. They created the bookshelves using scraps of old wood, which gives the shelves abundant character, even without the amazing old books. Their incredible collections of antique tables, side cabinets, stained glass, and quilts bring depth and warmth to this expansive open space.

These vintage Indonesian doors, now hanging in Jennifer and Fred's guesthouse, have so much patina and handcrafted character that they are pieces of art. Used as the hall's closet doors, the long narrow space needs no other adornments. You can easily design rooms around vintage doors, whether they're used as art pieces, pantry doors, headboards, closet doors, or even bar tops or sides of an island.

impact piece. If I'm doing a living room, a large wall hanging or an incredibly unique coffee table can do the trick. If you want to include numerous large pieces, make sure that they can handle each other visually, because you need to be able to give your eyes a place to rest. Be careful not to overdo it with the large pieces, because they sometimes conflict with each other and diminish the dramatic impact that each piece creates.

Small Pieces of Material Put Together to Make a Statement

Small pieces, even scrap pieces, can make a big impact when placed together. Think small pieces of reclaimed wood put together to create an entire wall, or scrap pieces of marble on the top of an island to make a stunning work of art as well as a functioning surface. Mismatched

boat. These are the types of pieces you build a room around. When designing and decorating a room, I make sure I know in advance if I want to create a space around a large focal point piece. If I'm designing a kitchen, sometimes I let the countertop of the island be the big

Sometimes I get so involved in my design projects that I end up doing some of the construction work. I made this wall and sign during the Mad River Barn renovation project. After the building crew put up a beautiful sheetrock wall (level, straight, and perfect), I brought in pieces of wood that were pulled out of the original barn. Slowly but surely the wall went up (not as perfect or straight, but with much more character). I sealed it well then started drilling in the plumbing handles to create the word *BARN*. I had the amazing folks at Burnett Scrap Metals, in Hinesburg, Vermont, save me a bucket of old plumbing handles as they came in (of course, on the side of the bucket they wrote *crazy Joanne* as a reminder to set them aside for me). These small handles alone would not grab your attention. But together, layered on top of each other, they truly spell *big impact*, or does that say *barn*?

piles of tile can be turned into an incredible mosaic on the wall or floor of a bathroom. Recycled bottles can be used to make a chandelier, or old country store receipts can be used to paper an entire wall. When you're looking around and you see a bunch of small stuff, think about what big impact they might make if you put them all together.

Little Touches Make a Big Difference

I have a pair of salt and pepper shakers that sit by my coffeemaker, and every morning they make me smile. They are a tiny pair of gnome fellows, and I love them. We can never underestimate the power of the small touches and how they make us feel. What are the small changes you can

Big impact pieces appear throughout the guesthouse at Jennifer's Gardens, in Austin, Texas. This gorgeous antique door, placed on a barn door slider, separates the bedroom from a long hallway to the main living space. It's a functional piece as well as one of the main design aesthetic features in the room. Vintage and antique doors can also be used as tables or even headboards.

make to add character to your home or bring a smile to your face? It could be as simple as changing the exterior of a lamp or adding a decorative piece to your bathroom that makes it more intimate and enjoyable. Think about little ways you can make big statements. Small items are what we in the vintage and antique industry call *smalls*. Do you have a small that will bring you happiness?

Collecting and Displaying

People love the nostalgia of old things that remind them of their childhood, a neighborhood, or even a moment in time. As we find ourselves bringing things back into our homes from the 1800s, or the 1940s, 1950s, 1960s, and 1970s, we can't help but smile at the memories they conjure (okay, maybe not memories from the 1800s, but you get the point). But how do we bring these items back into our homes without our spaces looking like Grandma's house or a museum? How you use those items is the key to solving this problem. One example is

Think Differently

SOMETIMES CREATING YOUR OWN COLLECTION MEANS YOU HAVE TO THINK OUTSIDE THE BOX. For example, instead of hiding away your collection of vintage belts, you might wrap them around a vase, creating a unique floral arrangement. Think of other ways you can conceive design and decorating ideas out of things you already have. Those belts could just as easily be displayed along a wall in frames (like artwork) or even covering a beam in a living room. Spend some time thinking through ways you can display your favorite pieces. You'll be surprised by how many unique and dramatic ideas you'll come up with.

before

after

Using old cabinet knobs and doorknobs I picked up at Mason Brothers Architectural Salvage Warehouse, I created a window display that both reflects light beautifully and gives me a tiny bit of privacy on the lake side of my home. Using wire, old beads, and the knobs, you can easily make a piece that will go in front of a window to create just the right amount of privacy and openness. These old glass knobs and pulls are works of art in their own right, and they make a gorgeous collection no matter how you use them.

This beautiful woven kilim rug from Dash and Albert is hung on a wall in the game room at Mad River Barn. The wood was reclaimed from the property's renovation project. Behind the rug, hidden, is acoustical tile to help with the sound issues in the busy game room space. Not only does hanging textiles, tapestries, bedspreads, or the like provide a dramatic look, but it can really help with noise issues. Vintage kilim rugs (flat tapestry-woven carpets or rugs) are wonderful pieces to use as wall art because they are not as heavy as wool rugs with finished backing.

how you might use old pictures and frames. A traditional way to display them would be to place a picture here, a picture there—one on the mantel, one on the fireplace, a couple on the dresser . . . all spread out. But using and displaying vintage frames and pictures in unique ways, as I'll cover a bit later, not only boosts the wow factor, but it gives visitors more reason to look at the images instead of just walking by them.

People always laugh when I tell them the difference between hoarding and collecting is how things are displayed. But I'm totally serious! As a photo stylist by profession, I'm telling you, how you put pieces together makes a huge difference. So have some fun collecting; just make sure when you display items that you do it with a little bit of finesse. Here are a few simple techniques you can use to get started.

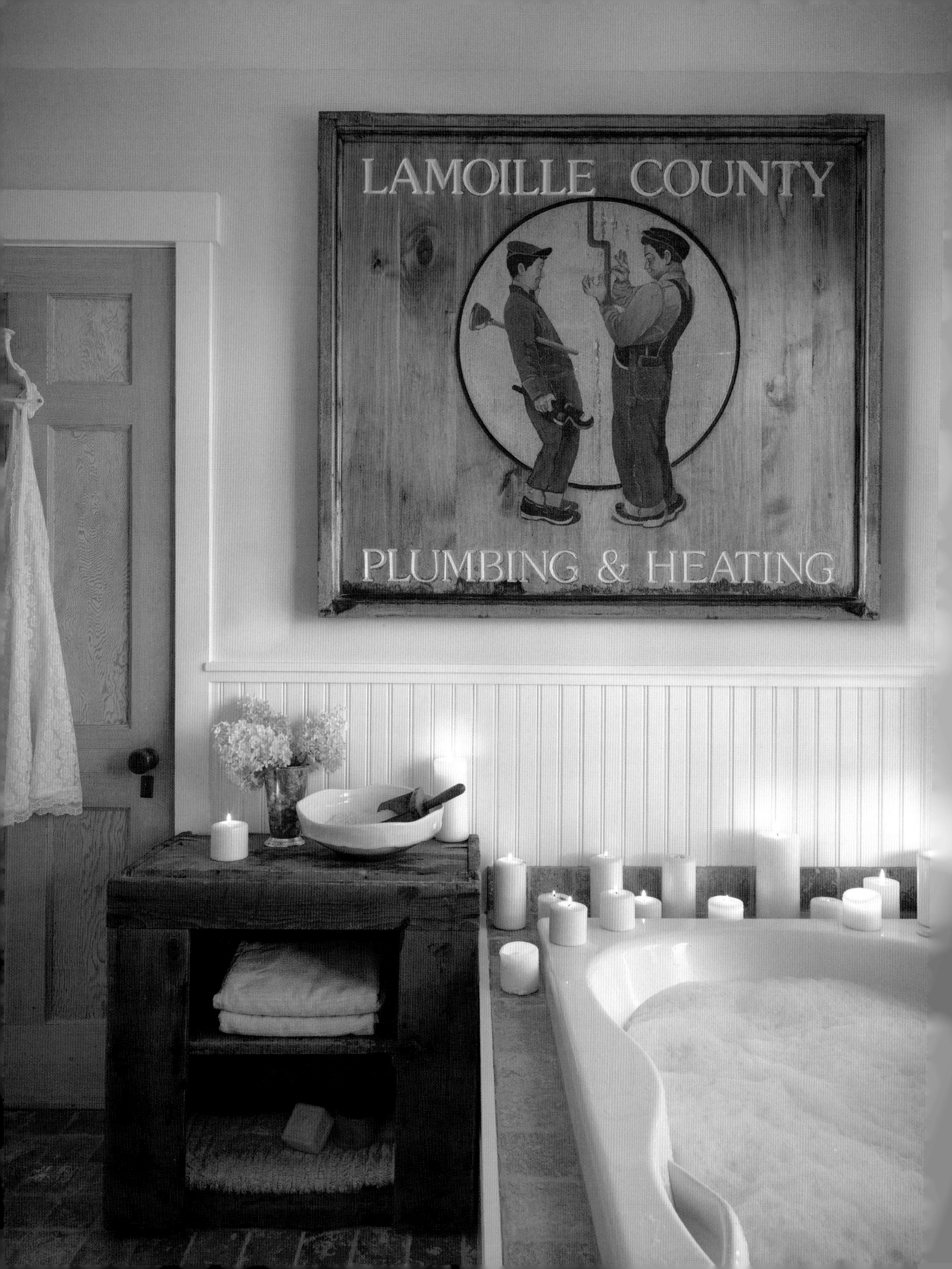
LAMOILLE COUNTY
PLUMBING & HEATING

Decide Your Look

First decide the look you want. Do you want a clean, modern look? Do you want a fun, eclectic space? Do you want to cover a lot of ground or a tiny area? Is your collection functional as well as aesthetic (think bowls, paintbrushes, hats, baskets)?

Going by Style

For a French country look, think creams, whites, and light blues. Want eclectic bohemian flair? Think green plants, bright colors, and flea market finds. For a modern farmhouse style, consider white shiplap, white tiles, warm woods, industrial touches, black frames, and white linens. Displaying and collecting by style lets you design your rooms in a variety of ways just by keeping the style theme the same.

A solid wooden shelving unit that used to be in a toolshed at the turn of the century now serves as a great side table in a modern bathroom. The sign, found at an antique shop in central Vermont, was the focal piece around which the other colors were added. Both of these pieces are big impact pieces but because the table is a natural color it blends in, allowing the vintage sign to stand out. The antique door was purchased at a salvage shop in New Hampshire. All the doors were stripped to their natural wood state and left as is. The tiling was created from leftover secondhand tiles found in a back room of a tile shop.

This shelving system is made from reclaimed wood that came out of the renovation project of this early-1800s farmhouse. With locally made custom wrought-iron brackets, this functional shelving unit shows off a collection of unique beers and liquors.

Going by Color

I have a friend who collects anything that is blue—a very specific blue. So when she sees a platter, a vase, or a pillow in that shade, she grabs it. When you're going by color, try to make sure that you're not

Above, left: Bev Martinets' bedroom is truly a place to relax. To the simple wood walls (she had stripped off the paint to let the original wood shine) she added elements to bring peace and tranquility to her room, like the vintage chenille bedspreads and pillow shams she found in Aspen, Colorado, and in Texas. Above the bed is a vintage JCPenney mirror. With natural light streaming in through the window, lined with sheers, the space is calming and inviting.

Above, right: Sometimes decorative displays get a point across. In the hallway of the Longhouse rooms of Mad River Barn, I made a sign from an old kitchen cabinet door that I had picked up at the ReSource Building Material Store, in Burlington, Vermont, for $5. I sanded the door a little bit to let the paint color underneath come through. Using letter stencils I added the wording and a sheep picture, then sealed it.

Opposite: Shannon Quimby's kitchen provides a nice example of how to style a collection. On a shelf above the stove, she placed her vintage bowling pins. Slowly, over the years, the collection has grown. The cabinets beyond the pins never get used so she doesn't mind hiding them. The antique porch brackets are nice touches on the sides of the stove hood, and the vintage grocery sign pulls all the colors together nicely. It doesn't take much to make the most of your collections, just a little bit of thought to how they might be displayed.

Styling this shot for Gardener's
Supply Company, in Burlington,
Vermont, to show off their lights and
plant tray, I used a soft blue antique
table, worn white shiplap wall, a lacy
cream-colored scarf, and an antique
metal bowl as the plant container.
Using materials that nod to the French
country design style, my goal was to
create a simple yet elegant display.

Paige and Smoot Hull used an old couch and chair from Paige's mother for The Vintage Round Top house in Round Top, Texas. They picked up some slipcovers at Target and added some custom pillows made out of vintage grain sacks to give the furniture pieces a cozy feel. The large garage sale trunk makes for a great coffee table. Not only is it useful, but it has amazing character and color. They have fun wondering about the wording around it, which hints at a military person's history. Trunks like these make for functional and visually appealing pieces. You can use them as coffee tables or bedside tables. If you want to raise them up, just add some hardware store bun feet or legs.

overwhelming your space. Perhaps you can keep your small collection on one shelf instead of on every horizontal surface in the room. If you have a variety of pillows, keep them on one bench instead of every chair in the room. Bunching works. A wall of black frames, a table of clear glass jars—alone they don't really stand out, but displayed together they make a powerful statement.

Going by Object

Working with one object, to create what we in the industry call a vignette (a powerful scene), is one way of making your spaces and objects feel more modern and current. Books are a great example of objects that can create a compelling vignette. You can easily display books on a wall of gorgeous bookshelves or on a modern picture rail that allows

a.fter

A wall of reclaimed wood is a great way to make a big change with just a couple of days of labor. This once-plain dining room was transformed with about $100 worth of old tongue-and-groove wood paneling and some serious effort. I purchased the reclaimed wood at the ReSource Building Material Store, in Burlington, Vermont. I brought it home, cleaned it well, and then painted the pieces with a very watered-down whitewash. A construction crew spent a day putting the wall up (making sure to screw the boards into the studs). I added a custom-made farmhouse table that was made from old floorboards and porch posts. Secondhand mismatched chairs work well in the space. I picked up the vintage 1970s chandelier at Habitat for Humanity and replaced the glass globe pieces with some Edison bulbs to give it a more trendy look. This dining room style has been totally turned around.

before

Left: Bev Martinets' personal bathroom in her bed and breakfast has some lovely little touches. Next to the vintage tub is a unique piece that is a wonderful spot to place candles and bath salts. This bathroom provides a romantic spa-like feeling, which is perfect after a long and busy day.

Right: Along Shannon's staircase are vintage baluster tops. These striking architectural features are mini pieces of sculptural art that are touched and loved every day. By keeping her railing design clean and contemporary, the vintage pieces with various colors and patinas, going up three flights of stairs, stand out and get noticed. Balusters can usually be found at architectural salvage shops.

the books to face the room. And you can stack them in piles against a wall to create an eclectic and hip display. Or instead of having three different small bookshelves in the room, try to create one big display location.

Rule of Three

When designing a space with your collections, odds work better than evens. When putting together a table display, for example, sets of 7, 11, or 13 always look beautiful. An exception to this principle would be if you're going for a more modern chromatic look. One way to achieve this look is by placing four paintings of the exact same size across a wall.

Lizzy and Luis found this safe in a vintage furniture store in Portland, Oregon. It was the first piece of furniture they actually bought together. They thought it would be perfect for a nightstand, before they realized how heavy it was. Thankfully, the store owner offered to deliver it. They hoped to find a million dollars in it, but no such luck. But it is "safe" to say, that piece looks amazing in their guest bedroom—and it's not moving for a while.

THE NEWS FROM PARAGUAY → LILY TUCK

LEAN IN | SHERYL SANDBERG

Punnett Safe Co.
ROCHESTER. N.Y.

Above: My friend Shannon Quimby loves little things, like tiny porcelain deer, little frames, or rolls of yarn. She is a collector. When her new house was built (most of it out of old materials), she had a shelving unit made to display all her little finds and frames. As a designer and stylist, she has a great eye for how to put things together. Vintage glass knobs add some whimsy to the small drawers.

Left: Karen and Patrick Kenny of South Porch Antiques, which can be found online, are well known for their gorgeous displays at their fair booths. Here, at the Country Living Fair in Atlanta, Karen shows off items they found or repurposed themselves in distinctive and creative ways. Notice how the various collections of cream colors, whites, natural woods, and metal work with a couple pops of color thrown in. When you visit retail shops, fairs, and antique shows, check out how they display their collections. You'll get some great ideas for how you can do it at home.

after

In a rental property in Stowe, Vermont, I got a little more creative in using salvage. Here I used vintage shutters and industrial antique desk lamps (rewired) to create a snug bed alcove. I reused the side table dressers that were already there, which look totally different in the space now. An old door serves as the headboard and an old chest found at a recycle center serves as the suitcase stand. The contemporary wall vinyl of sheep pops against these age-old materials, giving this bedroom a fun, boutique hotel feel.

before

after

For me, renovating is not just about adding unique features to a space and bringing it back to life, it's also about allowing the old materials to be reused by someone else. Everything in this kitchen, including the curtains and blinds, was either put on Craigslist and sold or donated to the local rebuild/recycling centers. Take the time to find out where your old things can go. Donate, sell, or give away materials that can be used in a renovation project. The dumpster should be your last resort.

before

In only a few simple steps and one afternoon, you can turn an old board into a coatrack. Using napkins (ripped into pieces), decoupage them onto the board. Then sand, seal, and add some fun brackets. I love these deer-head brackets I picked up at a HomeGoods store. You can use vintage knobs, cabinet handles, antique hooks, or whatever you like. This romantic coatrack goes wonderfully with my recycled vintage fabric TOTeM Salvaged handbag.

How to Create a Coatrack with Decorative Napkins and Brackets

1. Choose a board and cut to the desired size of the coatrack.
2. Collect decorative paper napkins and rip into pieces.
3. Decoupage napkin pieces onto board.
4. Let dry.
5. Sand and seal board with polyurethane.
6. Let dry.
7. Add brackets to front of board.
8. Hang on wall and hang your coats.

This tiny corner in the offices of HMC Advertising became a space where I created a little reading nook. The vintage chair I picked up at Habitat for Humanity, and I used a modern wool plaid to reupholster it. The bookshelves are made from reclaimed wood and hardware store piping. It takes a while to get all the pipes level (after a bit of twisting and turning). Once set, the boards can be laid across them. This bookshelf has floor flanges that are screwed into the ceiling to keep it from moving. If you find unthreaded metal piping at a rebuild center or scrap yard, it's easy to get the ends threaded (so you can screw in the floor flanges or elbows). Just call around to plumbing or piping shops and see who does it. I used old printer block letters to create the words on the wall, words the employees gave me as examples of what inspires them.

after

These lamps were once in the cottages at Basin Harbor, on Lake Champlain, Vermont. They languished in the storage rooms and attics for several years, gathering dust. They were good lamps with nice shapes, but they just didn't give the aesthetic feel we were going for while renovating the cottages. At the marina we asked for any lines not being used on the boats. With a little time and some hot glue, these lamps were totally transformed into works of art. Basic lamps are so easy to find at secondhand shops. Lines, wire, shells, broken pieces of tile, or any number of small things can transform an outdated 1970s or 1980s lamp. You could also try dictionary pages, floral napkins, or peel-off letters or numbers.

before

Left: Lizzy and Luis had long been admirers of designers Chelsea and Brandt Kaemingk, of Make King, and they knew they wanted a Make King home. In this bathroom, the designers blended traditional and modern touches. Using the vintage table with a vessel sink instead of a drop-in allowed them to keep the space under the table open. That, in turn, made visible the back wall of beautiful white tile. This touch helps lend an airy and expansive feel to the space. Keeping the color palette neutral grounds the space while also allowing the vintage piece to take center stage. The vintage light fixtures all have a custom, unlacquered brass finish, which was done by the designers themselves. Vessel sinks are a great way to use vintage tables (instead of dressers) for bathroom vanity tops.

Right: In their warehouse-turned-home, Carol and Randy Dupree used what was originally the front door of the building as the door into the guest bedroom. It had layers of paint on it, but using a grinder with a piece of high-grit sandpaper, they brought it back to the original red color then sealed it. They hung it on a track to make it easy to open and not lose any space in the room for a door swing. The vintage dresser was found at an antique shop. The windows above were found on the street; Someone was throwing them away during a remodeling project. Though these bits and pieces are diverse, the place is beautifully put together.

before

after

before

When opportunity knocks, answer. I was helping a friend look at an old country store counter when in the same backyard I spotted this wooden blue shelving piece. We got it to her house, and during a very budget-friendly renovation in her bathroom, we added it above the toilet. When you see big-impact pieces like these at unusual places, don't be afraid to ask if they would be willing to part with them. You just never know. We also used reclaimed lath (very thin pieces of wood), which we found at an architectural shop, as a place to hang hooks and keep wet towels off the sheetrock. We fit the lath above the trim, whitewashed it and sealed it, and then added the modern hooks. Both of these of salvaged pieces add character to this suburban home without costing a lot.

This countertop area next to the sink shows the effort that Fred and Jennifer took to create a guesthouse that really speaks to their love of art. The counters are made from concrete and recycled glass fragments, pieces of old bracelets, necklaces, pressings from plants, and even pieces of glass from car wrecks. The character of these counters are just one of the many details to behold. The gorgeous old wood came from Fred's home that had burned down. He salvaged the wood and stored it for more than 25 years. This Austin, Texas, guesthouse is filled with details, vintage finds, and small touches that make it unique.

Creating an eclectic display can be practical as well as pretty. During my own kitchen renovation, we decided not to have any upper cabinetry and instead make an extra-large island that would hold all our cutlery and dishware. Building the island with open shelving allowed me to display my vintage and antique finds, such as the bowls, plates, glassware, and cutting boards I've picked up at secondhand shops, antique stores, and flea markets. I'm a sucker when I travel to Italy. I head straight to the flea markets and look for the vintage linen tablecloths that sell for only a few Euros. One of my green glass pitchers was my grandmother's, so I started collecting more of them. I love that they are easy to access and look great in my open shelving. Each time I use one of these items, I'm filled with delight from all my experiences, memories, and finds. Our island, truly the heart of our home, is custom built with a top made from salvaged wood that we picked up from a farmer who also collects old wood. These very thick pieces (which you need for a large island) are Douglas fir. They were once floor joists from an 1800s railroad building. It makes me wonder about the people who walked across those floorboards in their time of use. What railroad journey were they taking, and did they enjoy themselves along the way?

before

after

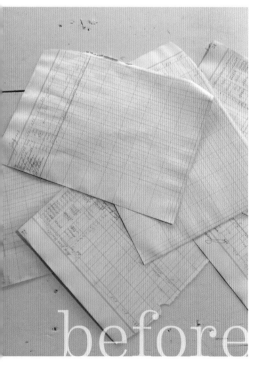

before

It was a blast to create this table vignette at Paige and Smoot Hull's home in Round Top, Texas. I brought with me a bunch of old ledger pages from a 1920s antique ledger, a black-and-white scarf from Goodwill, as well as a variety of glass jars, vases, and brass candleholders. I laid the pages down on the table in a random pattern, making sure that a little bit would peek out from the edges of the scarf, then I laid down the scarf. After that I randomly placed the glass vases and the candleholders. I moved them around a bit to make sure the different height levels were spread out evenly. Using the same color flowers (here I used various pinks), the ensemble came together beautifully. This is a very affordable and fun way to create a tablescape.

Left: During my eight-part video series *Designing & Decorating with Salvage*, for DIY Network, I was working in this room to redo a fireplace. While there, we spruced up the rest of the space. To do that, I made a coffee table out of salvaged pieces. I found the base at a secondhand store, and I picked up a blue painted vintage door at Restoration Resources, in Boston. I had a piece of tempered glass cut to fit the top. Once the door was cut to size, I easily attached the base of the old coffee table. I sealed the blue tabletop, then added the glass. On top of the table I put together a simple display using a vintage silver tray and some pieces that Patty and Rob, the homeowners and producers of the videos, already owned. Look around and see what you already have to create your own table display.

Right: As an expert on salvage, Shannon Quimby has an incredible eye for how to put pieces together. Here, she used an old gate as a headboard, turned an old vintage table lamp into a hardwired wall sconce, and used a small antique butcher-block table as her bedside stand. On the stand are some trinkets and vases that mean a great deal to her, including a vintage frame with a picture of the two of us at the seaside. Put pieces that mean something to you in your bedroom, next to your bed, so that you'll wake up and go to sleep to these special items.

Left: Carol and Randy Dupree really own the key to style. Their Georgia warehouse-turned-home is filled with collections, including locks that Randy picked up here and there. The metal spiral staircase that heads to Carol's sewing loft came from a bar in Gainesville, Florida, and was purchased on Craigslist.

Right: Cara and her family redid their Portland, Oregon, basement to make a cozy place to hang out. To warm it up, Cara added reclaimed wood from an old barn that was deconstructed in Washington state and sold by the Barnwood Boyz, in Vancouver, Washington. She hand selected the pieces, choosing some with the old barn paint showing, to give the wall the authentic look and feel of the old barn wood. They even lined the deep sill window with wood, making it feel more like a piece of wall art than a cellar window. The Barcelona chair was a lucky garage sale find, which was re-strapped. The vintage midcentury couches go beautifully with the new West Elm chair and the Jøtul gas stove, which really keeps it super cozy down in the basement, no matter what the season.

I created this table for HMC Advertising using basic lumber for the legs and skirt. I then added a sign I found at the scrap metal yard (turning it upside down) and gave it a fun layer of duct tape. I dented up some of my old soup cans, added some more duct tape, and put in some plants for an eclectic industrial look. The old paper slicer I found at a secondhand shop (I removed the scary blade). Put together, with the hip plaid wool pillow I made from Johnson Woolen Mills fabric and HMC's own couch (that they had in an upstairs office), this one-time garage bay is fun and funky—a perfect place for the HMC creative team to come up with some brilliant ideas for their clients.

7

Functional and Fantastic Design Ideas

Ways to Make the Most of Your Usable Home Pieces

Whatever your space, be it a house, condo, apartment, flat, or cottage, you can find ways to add personal pieces that also serve important functions for your daily living. With style and finesse, you can add useful items from vintage and recycled goods to the kitchen, dining, living, bathroom, and bedroom areas of your home, filling each space with character and soul without all the clutter and mess sometimes associated with salvage materials. This chapter demonstrates how functional pieces, such as countertops, light fixtures,

This kitchen island in Lizzy and Luis's Mount Tabor, Oregon, home started with the legs, which they believe once belonged to a large dining table. The designers, Chelsea and Brandt Kaemingk at Make King, found them in a salvage shop in Washington state. They then used reclaimed wood to build the new table around them. The bottom shelf not only serves to hold large pots and pans, but it brings up the height of the piece, which was necessary because the legs were not at counter height. The large apron (the piece placed at a right angle on the underside of the countertop) shows off the character of the reclaimed wood. This same wood can also be seen in the backsplash along the underside of the window. This masterpiece takes center stage in the living space. It's the first thing you see when you open the front door, and it is a perfect example of how to turn a functional piece into a stunning design feature.

vanities, dressers, and dining tables, can also be your design highlights. As you'll see, when function meets reclaimed design, you don't need much else.

Kitchen

Everything in a kitchen can be made from salvage, recycled, and vintage materials. A few of my favorite uses for reclaimed material include storage, islands, countertops, lighting, and doors. Old pine cupboards can serve as a pantry or can become open shelving for bowls and dishes. If you are hunting for shelving and see a vintage cupboard you like, take a closer look. Maybe you can take the door off the cupboard and use it for open shelving. Or perhaps you could use that door to make a sign or a table, or something else.

Small islands can be helpful in a kitchen that's not large enough for a full-blown island. Small kitchen islands can be made out of vintage butcher-block tables, or even a piece of scrap marble set upon a custom-made base. For larger islands, I try to find an old country store counter. These old-fashioned counters,

especially those with open shelving or bins on the back side, can make an amazing statement piece. Many times, old countertops or old desks are not at counter height but you can raise them up by adding a toe kick area (which is also a nice feature). You can even add a larger top to an existing base to give yourself a bar seating area. A large dining table works for a kitchen island as well, just add a shelf on the bottom to create more storage and bring up the height.

Task lights over your kitchen countertop don't have to be boring, but they should provide direct light onto the counter or island. Pick out

During the renovations of The Vintage Round Top, a vacation home and rental in Round Top, Texas, Paige and Smoot Hull donated all the materials they removed to Habitat of Humanity. Once the space was cleared out, they were able to start putting it back together with collected salvaged pieces. One day Paige was driving down the road and she saw a large tabletop board at Hector the Collector's side-of-the-road stand. She learned that the piece had once been the top of a dining table for a traveling carnival. When the carnival was on the road they would just throw it in their van, and then set it up on saw horses for an instant dining table. The strong man, bearded lady, and the sword swallowers all sat around this piece of wood, eating their meals, moving from city to city. Paige and Smoot loved the story and enjoy sharing it with their visitors. The rest of the space is filled with other antique pieces they have found throughout their travels in Texas.

some vintage lights where the bulb is facing down (think semi-flush fixtures, or pendants).

For a small kitchen, a swing door for a pantry closet takes up a lot of valuable space. A barn door slider works very well as an alternative to a swing door, even for pantries that are as narrow as a bookshelf. Find an exceptional door with lots of character to be the highlight of your space. Don't overlook inexpensive hollow-core doors (you know, the doors that you can easily kick a hole through like a Hollywood stuntperson because there is nothing in the middle). Apply a coat of chalk paint to create a chalkboard door that you can use for writing grocery lists.

Living Room

Vintage leather club chairs, quality heirloom pieces that can be reupholstered, or even some showstopper antiques are all you need in a living room space. I'm also big on old rugs with lots of color,

Changing Perceptions

WHEN I'M HIRED AS A DESIGNER, I BRING LOTS OF VINTAGE, SALVAGE, AND REPURPOSED MATERIALS INTO A PROJECT. Clients often start to see things differently and start telling me about the things they have recycled or repurposed at home. I welcome the chance to share my enthusiasm and passion, and give people a better understanding of these materials. I love the fact that people contact me because they want to bring in old things and reclaimed materials, and they appreciate how I use them in my unique designs. But no matter why I'm hired, I also try to speak to the home and the owners. Am I representing them? For example, if the project is decorating an older lakefront cottage, I might seek out items that would have been seen in same cottage 50 or 100 years ago, but at the same time I have to make sure those items bring a smile to the owners' faces. Because if it's not fun, why do it?

after

Every salvaged and vintage element of this updated bathroom is a functional piece. An old turkey feeder has been turned into a light, the sink is recycled, the trash can is a vintage maple bucket, and the vanity is made from reclaimed wood and old piping. The towel hook and the toilet paper holder were made from piping that came out of an old building during the renovation project. Blended with modern touches, such as the porcelain floor tile, subway tile, wall-to-wall mirror, and fun shower curtain, this bathroom at the Mad River Barn Inn shows how function and style can go very well together and give the guests plenty to look at and admire while they're in the room.

before

You have to admire a well-done upholstering job. It can take a lot of work, but these amazing vintage 1960s stools, redone by Revive Upholstery & Design, in Portland, Oregon, with high-end leather and wool, are works of art as well as functioning bar stools. If you have great furniture, or even better, if your parents or grandparents have amazing vintage pieces, getting them reupholstered is well worth it.

because they can tie a space together. If you're looking for more affordable and eclectic solutions, then consider using trunks or pallets as coffee tables, or just grab some vintage white bedspreads from your local secondhand shop and slipcover your current couch.

Dining Room

Lighting can always be a game changer in a dining room. Look for large vintage chandeliers or cool industrial pendants to make a statement. Make sure that your ceiling is braced to handle the additional weight of these fixtures. Next to these pieces, everything else should stay simple and clean looking.

Older tables can be found everywhere, or you can custom make your own with reclaimed wood. Six or eight matching chairs are sometimes hard to find. Consider mixing and matching chairs by a color (all pink or all black, for

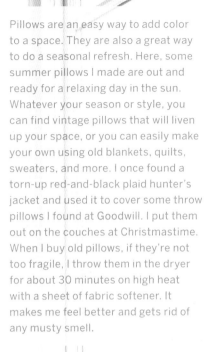

Pillows are an easy way to add color to a space. They are also a great way to do a seasonal refresh. Here, some summer pillows I made are out and ready for a relaxing day in the sun. Whatever your season or style, you can find vintage pillows that will liven up your space, or you can easily make your own using old blankets, quilts, sweaters, and more. I once found a torn-up red-and-black plaid hunter's jacket and used it to cover some throw pillows I found at Goodwill. I put them out on the couches at Christmastime. When I buy old pillows, if they're not too fragile, I throw them in the dryer for about 30 minutes on high heat with a sheet of fabric softener. It makes me feel better and gets rid of any musty smell.

Because of today's thick mattresses and tall bed heights, antique dressers make for useful bedside tables. Not only are they the right height, but they provide lots of room for books, a lamp, and collectibles. These dressers are in abundance at antique and vintage shops and will add style, character, and storage to your bedrooms. This hand-painted toile-work dresser is in Kim and Cliff Deetjen's bedroom. Kim loves having the larger bedside table for personal items. Another antique dresser, of a slightly different size and look, flanks the bed on Cliff's side. It also adds tons of storage to the room.

During the renovation of this guest room bathroom, the outdated wall-to-wall cabinetry was donated and new double pedestals were brought in. Mirrors are framed in old barn wood, while new light fixtures have vintage glass shades to add a little more personality and quirkiness to this powder room.

example, no matter the make or style of chair) or by a materials scheme (such as all wood chairs with varied patinas, finishes, and colors).

Bedroom

Two of my favorite ways to change the look of a bedroom are with the headboard and bedside tables. Vintage dressers and large trunks are simple ways to add storage and function next to the bed. And headboards can be a place to get really creative—think large slabs of

old-growth reclaimed wood with tons of character, an old door, a vintage blanket hanging on a rod, or shutters lined up behind the bed. Whatever your choice, just make sure vintage woods are cleaned well and sealed on all sides.

Bathroom

Vintage tubs are really fun, but many people shy away from them because they worry about rusting, especially the cast-iron feet. These worries may be well founded, because

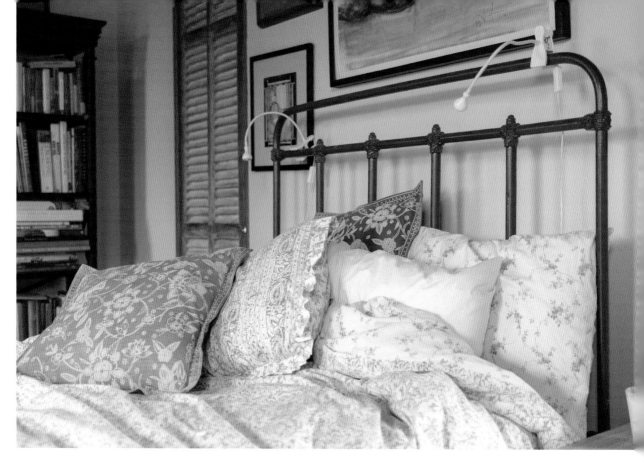

Often when we think about old cast-iron or wrought-iron beds, we think shiny and wobbly brass, but here Jennifer and Fred show us that you can change up your bed frame with a more modern color, such as a charcoal brown. You can also stabilize older bed frames by tightening all the loose bolts, using either thread-locking adhesives or adding a plate at the corners. The other touches, such as antique doors, vintage prints, sumptuous pillows, and books, make this a cozy, curl-up-and-relax type of bedroom.

the feet are usually the first thing to rust off. But there's no need to worry about smaller nicks on the rest of an enameled tub, as they're pretty easy to fix. As for any rusted feet, they can always be removed and some gorgeous blocks of reclaimed beams can be placed under the tub to create a more modern look. I'm also a huge fan of vintage mirrors. Not only do the frames add a lot of character, but the older mirrors somehow always make me look better; I leave my bathroom feeling like a million bucks! And as you've seen throughout this book, I love to turn vintage tables and dressers into vanities. Doing this is not as hard as you might think, and the finished piece can transform a space.

Seattle artist Michelle de la Vega has an eye for interior design. With a tiny budget, she renovated an outdated kitchen into a striking industrial-style space. She picked up the sink and the shelf brackets at Second Use, in Seattle, Washington. She added a vintage green light fixture and used reclaimed wood for shelving, which warmed up the room. Because of the open shelving and extra-large sink, the space looks larger than it actually is and everything she needs is within reach. Large vintage sinks are some of my favorite functional design pieces. Not only can you fill them with days' worth of dishes, but a bold and beautiful sink becomes a showpiece in your kitchen.

Above: Bev Martinets' kitchen is pretty busy in the morning. When she needs something, she wants it to be readily available, but she also wants it to look good. As an avid collector and cook, it's not surprising that many of her vintage finds are functional items she can use in her kitchen every day. She picked up the green shelving unit at an auction many years ago for $60, the candy molds are from a garage sale, and the vintage Mexican plates once belonged to her uncle. She collected the copper pots and cutting boards over time at estate sales and antique fairs. Fun, unique, and useful vintage kitchen tools are hard for her to pass up. Luckily, she has a great place to display them, and she uses them all regularly.

Left: You don't have to spend years at flea markets or antique shops to create your own functional display. This instant pantry is perfect for tiny homes, campers, cottages, or little apartments. Without the swing of a door, more room is available for storage, and you can see what you have in an instant. Here I created a cohesive look by using recycled glass jars (my cousins, Toni and Tommy, save the large glass pickle jars for me from their restaurant) that I applied chalk paint to and then labeled.

Above: Every vintage, salvaged, and recycled piece in Paige and Smoot Hull's master bedroom at The Vintage Round Top, is not only exceptionally eye-catching, but also serves a purpose. The mirror, purchased at Old World Antieks, reflects the light from the bathroom window and serves as the full-length mirror in the room. The headboard is made from salvaged pieces from the Round Top Antique Show, and the recycled glass jug lamp is a good size for nighttime reading. The antique side table was picked up at another salvage shop. The door to the bathroom, which hangs on a barn door slider, was purchased at August Antiques, in Houston. The vintage bedspread is a perfect companion on chillier nights. This clean and stylish room is a great example of how functional pieces can also be used as the actual decor.

I do have a few collection weaknesses. Cutting boards, cream-colored pitchers, boots, and tables are all hard for me to resist. And though I'm trying to cut back on tables, because I'm running out of space, I still keep picking up the rest. As a stylist I can never have too many cutting boards, so I feel pretty good about it! Someday, I'll get a restaurant design project and do an entire wall of them. What is your favorite kitchen collection piece?

I spotted this old painted dresser at ReSource, in Burlington, Vermont, tucked between oak file drawers and some faux wood shelving. You have to really look for gems like these, and be willing to snag them the moment you see them. When I saw this dresser and its mirror on the floor, wrapped in a tarp, I instantly knew I wanted to make a bathroom vanity out of it. The top had some wear, but that was fine with me because I planned to cut a hole in it for a small drop-in sink. Remember, when you're dropping in a sink, measure carefully to be sure that the hole does not cut into the outside wood pieces that create the structural frame of the dresser. So measure your bowl size and keep that size in mind when looking for the right old furniture piece. Sometimes you'll need to make the drawers into half drawers, depending on how the plumbing is routed and the type of sink you use. A vessel sink, for example, needs much less space than a drop-in sink. Once you get the basics down on how to place a sink, you'll find that the carpentry itself is quite easy to do on your own. You can leave the plumbing work to a professional.

after

before

This outdated bathroom in the ski country of Stowe, Vermont, was in need of a face-lift. The design intent was to create a "boutique hotel style" rental property that stood out from the rest in a strong rental market. Adding simple paneling to the back wall, painting it, and then placing the dresser-turned-vanity in the spot where the old plumbing used to be instantly gave this bathroom a funky update that was functional for the homeowners and their rental guests. The mirror that once sat on the dresser was placed on the wall instead of back on the dresser. Before the sink was dropped in, we gave the top a two-part sealer to keep it from holding the moisture of any standing water. This dramatic character piece allowed us to keep the rest of the space simple and clean, while giving it a "photograph-worthy" style for those searching for fun rental properties in the area. If you rent out your property using an online service, look at functional salvage ideas that can both make your property stand out and be able to handle the wear and tear of rental guests.

We had some leftover whitewashed wood from the dining-room wall paneling project, so we used it to create a mini-bookshelf area. We took pieces of dark-stained reclaimed wood, cut them into shelves, and attached them to the paneling. This was a simple project, but it really added some character and function to the space.

I love using stone for countertops, but sometimes it can be just too expensive for budget projects. In such cases, I like to use vintage pieces of chalkboard slate or large pieces of stone tiles I find at salvage shops and stone yards. This old-school chalkboard slate now serves as the extra-deep countertop in a kitchen I designed for Heather and Andrew Lynds. I found the large pieces at an architectural salvage shop in central Vermont, and the tiler cut them into specific sizes to fit the counter and created a false front to make it look thicker than it actually is. You can make thin pieces of slate, or any other small pieces of stone for that matter, appear thicker by gluing on a false front. When you go into a salvage shop and find a lot of different-sized pieces, see if there is enough to create your own 24" × 24" tile pieces, or whatever size you need, that will cover the entire counter. Just butt them up against each other and join them with a clear caulking and you will hardly see a seam. Be sure to pick stone pieces that have the same thickness so as to create a smooth surface.

after

Headboards come in all shapes, sizes, and colors. At the Mad River Barn, the headboards not only serve as functioning pieces, which are easy to clean because of the faux leather, but they also become decorative focal points in the guest rooms. These types of headboards are very easy to make and are affordable. To make one, simply pick up a piece of reclaimed plywood at your local rebuild center and cut it to the size and shape you want. Add a wooden cleat to the back of the plywood so that you can hang it from the wall when the time comes. Then wrap the board in recycled carpet padding, which you can pick up at your local hardware store. Using a heavy-duty staple gun, staple it to the back. Then wrap your fabric around in the same way, once again stapling to the back. You can use faux leather, a vintage wool blanket, a quilt, or a woven rug—there are lots of unique colors, patterns, and styles to choose from in vintage textiles.

before

Fun, funky, eclectic, charming—I
could go on and on about this open
room plan for the guest cottage at
Jennifer's Gardens in Austin, Texas.
They've made the cottage feel so
inviting by using age-old materials
that already have a sense of life to
them. It can be felt through the patina,
textures, and depths of the materials,
such as the vintage pottery from
Mexico, the reclaimed wood on the
island, the recycled Chicago brick, and
the island top made from concrete
and recycled materials. A gigantic
antique Indonesian mirror reflects lots
of light into the room while showing
off the antique entrance doors. The
Mexican tile backsplash is made from
compressed concrete with hand-
painted stencils. The reclaimed wood-
and-piping shelving gives a little bit of
an industrial flair to the space while
making it easy for guests to know
where all the dishware is located. This
is a great space for a gathering, and
all of the unique touches and finds will
easily keep everyone talking!

The island in this renovated Stowe, Vermont, kitchen was once a wall separating the kitchen from the living space. Because of the loss of upper cabinets, I designed the island to have cabinetry on both sides, as well as a bar-style seating area, making the island the heart of the house. A wall was built to tuck away the refrigerator, add a pantry, and hide the plumbing that went upstairs, adding character as well as function. Gorgeous 100 percent recycled Fireclay tiles, from their Debris Series, were added, along with reclaimed 1700s wood for shelving. This wall now serves as functional decor. Not only does it hold all the glassware, but it gives this kitchen a whole lot more character.

It took only a handful of items to make this dining room feel special. A gorgeous live-edge table made from reclaimed wood, midcentury chairs, a vintage three-tiered pendant chandelier, and some personal artwork transformed this space. The designers of the home's renovation project, Make King, brought in the chandelier, and the homeowners, Lizzy and Luis, provided the artwork. Sometimes it's best to let the beauty and elegance of a few pieces stand out, and lighting can play a large role in doing that. Whether you're looking for task lighting that helps you see what you're doing, ambient lighting to create subtle background moods, or accent lighting that highlights something specific like a painting on a wall, you'll find many options in vintage lighting shops, secondhand places, and architectural salvage shops. An overhead chandelier on a dimmer plays all three roles, making it both a pretty piece and a very functional one. Lighting is often overlooked even though it is one of the most important aspects of your rooms. Think about the type of lighting you need, and then see if you can find an appropriate repurposed, vintage, or recycled piece that also fits your decorating style.

Left: This antique desk and chair in one of Bev Martinets' guest bedrooms at her bed and breakfast serves two functions. It's a nightstand for the cozy bed, which is layered with vintage spreads, bed skirt, and pillows, and it is also a practical desk for the many guests who bring their laptops or tablets. In bedrooms, which tend to be smaller than other rooms, using a vintage desk as a nightstand is a great way to combine functional needs.

Opposite: When designing this room for Mad River Barn, I knew that I would be filling it with recycled and reclaimed materials that came out of the original space during the renovation as well as numerous vintage finds. The platform bed is made with reclaimed beams, the small table and headboard are made from the building's old barn wood, and the pillow is made from the old wool blankets that used to be in the rooms. The side tables are reclaimed dimensional lumber, painted red, with offcuts of stone from the stone yard; the FLOR carpet squares are made from recycled materials; and the light fixture by Conant Metal & Light is made from old floor-lamp pieces. From the bedding company Dignify, the hand-stitched blankets are made from six layers of vintage sari cloth by women in high-risk situations in Bangladesh. These one-of-a-kind blankets are not only unique but help these women make a new life for themselves through a fair-trade work environment. It felt really great knowing that when ordering these blankets for every room in the inn we were helping these women get off the streets and rebuild their lives. Each and every salvaged design decision in these rooms was made with purpose, and the design has been a huge hit with the owners and the guests, proving that the hospitality industry can make a difference by the way it designs and reuses.

Resources to Get You Started

This sampling of resources is a basic overview of architectural salvage shops, rebuild centers, and other resources from the book. But they are only the tip of the iceberg. Secondhand markets, outdoor fairs, and urban flea markets have never been more abundant and varied. You only have to drive from Atlanta to Nashville to find more than a dozen antique malls along the way, or along Route 7 in Vermont to find dozens and dozens of amazing quaint shops. So it's important to do some real-time research before you head out on a trip. Check the papers for auctions, garage sales, and flea markets, because many folks who hold these types of sales still use the paper to announce their events. When I head out of town for a presentation or vacation, I always give myself an extra day to check out the area. I get online and research all the vintage shops, antique malls, fairs, flea markets, and Goodwill stores, and then I create my very own paper treasure map. Remember, don't forget to check their hours; I can't tell you how many times I've driven around on a Monday only to find that all the shops are closed on Monday and Tuesday.

As for the companies that create new products out of recycled materials, most of them sell online and will ship their products to you. So get a list together for all your "new" needs (carpeting, tile work, hardware) and search out the companies that use recycled materials in their products that best fit your needs and are closest to you. Many of these companies will send you samples for free or for a small fee.

Resource List

SAMPLING of FLEA MARKETS and FAIRS, SALVAGE SHOPS, STORES, and MATERIAL RESOURCE LOCATIONS MENTIONED in the BOOK

Building Materials Reuse Association		National	www.bmra.org
Craigslist		National	www.craigslist.org
Detroit Rug Restoration		National	www.detroitrugrestoration.com
Dignify		National	www.shopdignify.com
eBay		National	www.ebay.com
Etsy		National	www.etsy.com
Fireclay Tile		National	www.fireclaytile.com
Front Porch Forums		National	www.frontporchforum.com
Goodwill Stores		National	www.goodwill.org/locator
Habitat for Humanity ReStores		National	www.habitat.org/restores
The Loading Dock		National	www.loadingdock.org
Old House Online		National	www.oldhouseonline.com
National Flea Market Association		National	www.fleamarkets.org
The ReUse People of America		National	www.thereusepeople.org
The Salvation Army		National	www.salvationarmyusa.org
The Textile Trunk		National	www.textiletrunk.com
127 Corridor Sale		Multi-state	www.127sale.com
Country Living Magazine Fairs		Multi-state	www.countryliving.com/country-living-fair
Olde Good Things		Multi-state	www.ogtstore.com
Rejuvenation		Multi-state	www.rejuvenation.com

Please note that many of these locations sell their products online as well.

Southern Accents Architectural Antiques	Cullman	Alabama	www.antiques-architectural.com
Architectural & Garden Antiques	Fairhope	Alabama	www.rfantiques.com
Rescued Relics	Montgomery	Alabama	www.landmarkersfoundation.com/about-us/rescued-relics
Stardust Building Supplies	Glendale, Mesa, Phoenix	Arizona	www.stardustbuilding.org
Sweet Salvage	Phoenix	Arizona	www.sweetsalvage.net
Alameda Point Antiques Faire	Alameda	California	www.alamedapointantiquesfaire.com
Amighini Antique & Custom Doors	Anaheim	California	www.amighini.com
Ohmega Salvage	Berkeley	California	www.ohmegasalvage.com
Taipan Architectural Salvage	Carpinteria	California	www.taipanarchitecturalsalvage.com
Pasadena Architectural Salvage	Pasadena	California	www.pasadenaarchitecturalsalvage.com
Pasadena City College Flea Market	Pasadena	California	www.pasadena.edu/community/flea-market
Rose Bowl Flea Market and Market Place	Pasadena	California	www.rgcshows.com/RoseBowl.aspx
Architectural Salvage of San Diego	San Diego	California	www.architecturalsalvagesd.com
Treasure Island Flea	San Francisco	California	www.treasureislandflea.com
Builders Trading Company	San Marcos	California	www.builders-trading.com
Artefact Design & Salvage	Sonoma	California	www.artefactdesignsalvage.com
Center for ReSource Conservation	Boulder	Colorado	www.conservationcenter.org
Eron Johnson Antiques	Denver	Colorado	www.eronjohnsonantiques.com

Queen City Architectural Salvage	Denver	Colorado	www.localarchitecturalsalvage.com
Mile High Flea Market	Henderson	Colorado	www.milehighfleamarket.com
Irreplaceable Artifacts	Middletown	Connecticut	www.irreplaceableartifacts.com
Urban Miners	New Haven	Connecticut	www.urbanminers.com
The ReCONNstruction Center	Newington	Connecticut	www.reconnstructioncenter.org
United House Wrecking	Stamford	Connecticut	www.unitedhousewrecking.com
The Brass Knob Architectural Antiques	Washington	District of Columbia	www.thebrassknob.com
The Flea Market at Eastern Market	Washington	District of Columbia	www.easternmarket.net
ReUser Building Products	Gainesville	Florida	www.reuser.us/doors.html
Eco Relics	Jacksonville	Florida	www.ecorelics.com
American Salvage Miami	Miami	Florida	www.americansalvage.com
Lincoln Road Outdoor Antique & Collectable Market	Miami Beach	Florida	www.lincolnroadmall.info
Renninger's	Mount Dora, Melbourne	Florida	www.renningers.net
Tampa Bay Salvage	Palm Harbor	Florida	www.tampabaysalvage.com
Sarasota Architectural Salvage	Sarasota	Florida	www.sarasotasalvage.com
Architectural Accents	Atlanta	Georgia	www.architecturalaccents.com
Metropolitan Artifacts Inc.	Atlanta	Georgia	www.metropolitanartifacts.com
ReUse the Past	Grantville	Georgia	www.reusethepast.com
Pinch of the Past	Greensboro, Savannah, Madison	Georgia	www.pinchofthepast.com
Old House Society	Bloomington	Illinois	www.oldhousesociety.org

Architectural Artifacts	Chicago	Illinois	www.architecturalartifacts.com
Randolph Street Market Festival	Chicago	Illinois	www.randolphstreetmarket.com
Rebuilding Exchange	Chicago	Illinois	www.rebuildingexchange.org
Salvage One	Chicago	Illinois	www.salvageone.com
Urban Remains	Chicago	Illinois	www.urbanremainschicago.com
Jan's Antiques	Evanston	Illinois	http://jansantiques.net
Vintage Brick Salvage	Rockford	Illinois	www.bricksalvage.com
Wolff's Flea Market	Rosemont, Palatine	Illinois	www.wolffs.com
Kane County Flea Market	Saint Charles	Illinois	www.kanecountyfleamarket.com
White River Salvage	Centerville	Indiana	www.americanantiquities.com/ whiteriversalvage.html
fHg Architectural Salvage	Evansville	Indiana	www.fhgarchitecturalsalvage.com
Franklin Heritage Architectural Salvage	Franklin	Indiana	www.fhisalvage.org
Architectural Antiques of Indianapolis	Indianapolis	Indiana	www.antiquearchitectural.com
Doc's Architectural Salvage & Reclamation Services	Indianapolis	Indiana	www.docsarchitecturalsalvage.com
Shipshewana Auction & Flea Market	Shipshewana	Indiana	www.shipshewanatradingplace.com
Restoration Warehouse	Dubuque	Iowa	www.restorationwarehouse.net
Old Town Architectural Salvage	Wichita	Kansas	www.oldtownarchitecturalsalvage.com
Cowgirl's Attic/ Reclaimed Urban Artifacts	Lexington	Kentucky	www.cowgirlattic.com
Architectural Salvage, W. D. Inc.	Louisville	Kentucky	www.architecturalsalvage.com

The Bank Antique Architectural Elements	New Orleans	Louisiana	www.thebankantiques.com
The Green Project	New Orleans	Louisiana	www.thegreenproject.org
Ricca's Architectural Sales	New Orleans	Louisiana	www.riccasarchitectural.com
Architectural Antiquities	Harborside	Maine	www.archantiquities.com
The Old House Parts Company	Kennebunk	Maine	www.oldhouseparts.com
Portland Architectural Salvage	Portland	Maine	www.portlandsalvage.com
Housewerks Salvage	Baltimore	Maryland	www.housewerkssalvage.com
The Loading Dock	Baltimore	Maryland	www.loadingdock.org
Second Chance	Baltimore	Maryland	www.secondchanceinc.org
Community Forklift	Edmonston	Maryland	www.communityforklift.com
Boston Building Resources	Boston	Massachusetts	www.bostonbuildingresources.com
Building Materials Resource Center	Boston	Massachusetts	www.bostonbmrc.org
Old Bostonian	Boston	Massachusetts	www.oldbostonian.com
Restoration Resources	Boston	Massachusetts	www.restorationresources.com
Brimfield Antique Show	Brimfield	Massachusetts	www.brimfieldshow.org
Cambridge Antique Market	Cambridge	Massachusetts	www.marketantique.com
The Vintage Bazaar	Eliot	Maine	www.mybazaarlife.com
B &C Emporium	Allegan	Michigan	www.bandcallegan.weebly.com
Recycle Ann Arbor	Ann Arbor	Michigan	www.recycleannarbor.org
Architectural Salvage Warehouse of Detroit	Detroit	Michigan	www.aswdetroit.org
The Heritage Company	Kalamazoo	Michigan	www.heritagearchitecturalantiques.com
HeritageCo2	Royal Oak	Michigan	www.heritageco2.com
Salvage with Style	St. Joseph	Michigan	www.misalvagewithstyle.com

Materials Unlimited	Ypsilanti	Michigan	www.materialsunlimited.com
Architectural Antiques	Minneapolis	Minnesota	www.archantiques.com
Bauer Brothers Salvage	Minneapolis	Minnesota	www.bauerbrotherssalvage.com
City Salvage	Minneapolis	Minnesota	www.citysalvage.com
North Shore Architectural Antiques	Two Harbors	Minnesota	www.north-shore-architectural-antiques.com
Flowood Antique Flea Market	Flowood	Mississippi	www.flowoodantiquefleamarket.com
Old House Depot	Jackson	Mississippi	www.oldhousedepot.com
Cross Creek Architectural Artifacts	Springfield	Missouri	www.crosscreekartifacts.com
Architectural Salvage Inc.	Exeter	New Hampshire	www.oldhousesalvage.com
Nor'East Architectural Antiques	South Hampton	New Hampshire	www.noreast1.com
Recycling the Past	Barnegat	New Jersey	www.recyclingthepast.com
Amighini Architectural	Jersey City	New Jersey	www.amighini.net
Get a Grip & More	Washington	New Jersey	www.getagripandmore.com
Historic Albany Foundation	Albany	New York	www.historic-albany.org
Silver Fox Salvage	Albany	New York	www.silverfoxsalvage.com
Big Reuse	Astoria, Gowanus	New York	www.bigreuse.org
Shaver Brothers	Auburn	New York	www.shaverbrothers.com
Brooklyn Flea	Brooklyn	New York	www.brooklynflea.com
Reclaimed Home	Brooklyn	New York	www.reclaimedhome.com
Buffalo Reuse	Buffalo	New York	www.buffaloreuse.org
Finger Lakes ReUse	Ithaca	New York	www.fingerlakesreuse.org
Significant Elements	Ithaca	New York	www.significantelements.org
Zaborski Emporium	Kingston	New York	www.stanthejunkman.com
Artists and Fleas	New York	New York	www.artistsandfleas.com

Chelsea & Hell's Kitchen Flea Markets	New York	New York	www.annexmarkets.com/hells-kitchen-flea-market
Demolition Depot	New York	New York	www.demolitiondepot.com
Grand Bazaar NYC	New York	New York	www.grandbazaarnyc.org
Urban Archaeology	New York	New York	www.urbanarchaeology.com
New York Salvage	Oneonta	New York	www.newyorksalvage.net
Historic Houseparts	Rochester	New York	www.historichouseparts.com
ReHouse Architectural Salvage	Rochester	New York	www.rehouseny.com
Crossland Studio	Charlotte	North Carolina	www.realpages.com/sites/crossland/index.html
Preservation Greensboro	Greensboro	North Carolina	www.preservationgreensboro.org
Raleigh Flea Market	Raleigh	North Carolina	www.raleighfleamarket.net
The Stock Pile	Canton	Ohio	www.thestockpile.org
Wooden Nickel Antiques	Cincinnati	Ohio	www.woodennickelantiques.net
Old School Architectural Salvage Project	Cleveland	Ohio	216-496-1910
Columbus Architectural Salvage	Columbus	Ohio	www.columbusarchitecturalsalvage.com
Springfield Ohio Antique Show & Flea Market	Springfield	Ohio	www.springfieldantiqueshow.com
Toledo Architectural Artifacts Inc.	Toledo	Ohio	www.coolstuffiscoolstuff.com
Architectural Salvage Supply	Oklahoma City	Oklahoma	www.architecturalsalvagesupply.com
Buchanan Flea Markets	Oklahoma City	Oklahoma	www.buchananeventco.com
Aurora Mills Architectural Salvage	Aurora, Portland	Oregon	www.auroramills.com
Hippo Hardware & Trading Company	Portland	Oregon	www.hippohardware.com

Old Portland Hardware & Architectural	Portland	Oregon	www.oldportlandhardware.com
Christine Palmer & Associates	Portland	Oregon	www.christinepalmer.net
The Rebuilding Center of Our United Villages	Portland	Oregon	www.rebuildingcenter.org
Revive Upholstery & Design	Portland	Oregon	www.revivepdx.com
Salvage Works	Portland	Oregon	www.salvageworkspdx.com
Stars Antiques Malls	Portland	Oregon	www.starsantique.com
Antiques Capital, USA	Adamstown	Pennsylvania	www.antiquescapital.com
Architectural Emporium	Canonsburg	Pennsylvania	www.architectural-emporium.com
Saturday's Market	Middletown	Pennsylvania	www.saturdaysmarket.com
Architectural Antiques Exchange	Philadelphia	Pennsylvania	www.architecturalantiques.com
Philadelphia Salvage Company	Philadelphia	Pennsylvania	www.philadelphiasalvage.com
Provenance	Philadelphia	Pennsylvania	www.phillyprovenance.com
ReStore	Philadelphia	Pennsylvania	www.re-store-online.com
Construction Junction	Pittsburgh	Pennsylvania	www.constructionjunction.org
Historic York	York	Pennsylvania	www.historicyork.org
Bargain Hunters	Bristol, Johnson City, Knoxville	Tennessee	www.bargainhunterstn.com
South Front Architectural Antiques	Memphis	Tennessee	www.southfrontantiques.com
Garden Park Antiques	Nashville	Tennessee	www.gardenpark.com
Preservation Station	Nashville	Tennessee	www.thepreservationstation.com
Living Vintage	Alto	Texas	www.livingvintageco.com
Flown the Coop	Burton	Texas	www.2flownthecoop.com
Dallas Flea Markets	Dallas	Texas	www.buchananeventco.com/dallas.html
Discount Home Warehouse	Dallas	Texas	www.dhwsalvage.com

The Old Home Supply	Fort Worth	Texas	www.oldhomesupply.net
Discovery Architectural Antiques	Gonzales	Texas	www.discoverys.net
Adkins Antique Hardware Co.	Houston	Texas	www.adkinsantiques.com
Historic Houston	Houston	Texas	www.historichouston.org
Old World Antieks	La Grange	Texas	www.oldworldantieks.com
Junk Gypsy	Round Top	Texas	www.gypsyville.com
Round Top Antique Show	Round Top	Texas	www.roundtop.org/antique_show_info.php
Round Top Register	Round Top	Texas	www.roundtop.com
Old is Better Than New	San Antonio	Texas	www.old-sa.com
George's Salvage	Salt Lake City	Utah	www.georgessalvage.com
Barge Canal Market	Burlington	Vermont	802-497-7119
Conant Metal & Light	Burlington	Vermont	www.conantmetalandlight.com
ReSource Building Material Store	Burlington	Vermont	www.resourcevt.org
Vermont Farm Table	Burlington	Vermont	www.vermontfarmtable.com
Vintage Inspired Lifestyle Marketplace	Burlington	Vermont	www.vintageinspired.net
5 Corners Antiques	Essex Junction	Vermont	www.5cornersantiques.com
Architectural Salvage Warehouse	Essex Junction	Vermont	www.greatsalvage.com
Champlain Valley Antique Center	Shelburne	Vermont	www.vermontantiquecenter.com
Vermont Salvage	White River Junction	Vermont	www.vermontsalvage.com
Architectural Old House Parts	Front Royal	Virginia	www.oldhouseparts.net
Governor's Antiques and Architectural Materials	Mechanicsville	Virginia	www.governorsantiques.com
Caravati's Inc.	Richmond	Virginia	www.caravatis.com

Black Dog Salvage	Roanoke	Virginia	www.blackdogsalvage.com
ReBuild Warehouse	Springfield	Virginia	www.rebuildwarehouse.org
The RE Store	Bellingham	Washington	www.re-store.org
Bedrock Industries	Seattle	Washington	www.bedrockindustries.com
Earthwise Architectural Salvage	Seattle	Washington	www.ewsalvage.com
Fremont Sunday Market	Seattle	Washington	www.fremontmarket.com
Seattle Building Salvage	Seattle	Washington	www.seattlebuildingsalvage.com
Second Use	Seattle	Washington	www.seconduse.com
Elkhorn Antique Flea Market	Hales Corners	Wisconsin	www.nlpromotionsllc.com
DeConstruction, Inc.	Madison	Wisconsin	www.dcisalvage.com
Salvage Heaven	Milwaukee	Wisconsin	www.salvageheaven.com

Acknowledgments

The places I go, the people I meet, the stories I hear . . . this is what makes my work my passion. This is a world of talented people, and I want to thank you all for sharing your experience, expertise, homes, time, designs, and energy with me. I'm so grateful to be on this journey with you. If I have forgotten your name here, please forgive me and know that I appreciate your help to put this labor of love together. You all have empowered and amazed me . . . thank you! Friends, family, and a career I love—I couldn't ask for more—nor should I.

Once again, my dear friend and photographer SUSAN TEARE was my right-hand gal throughout this project. Thank you, Susan and your team, LINDSAY RAYMONDJACK and SUSAN BLACK-TURNER, for coming along on this journey, once again. There are a handful of pictures by other talented photographers as well: thank you to MARK GAYNOR, APRIL PIZANA, JEFF CLARKE, and GARY SWEETMAN for adding to the visual inspiration in this book. The places Susan and I went, the folks whom we now call friends . . . truly . . . thank you.

A big thank you to THE COUNTRYMAN PRESS, ANN TREISTMAN, RÓISÍN CAMERON, and DEVORAH BACKMAN for being so excited about this third book and helping me communicate my thoughts (basically making me look and sound good). It truly takes a village with me at the helm. Thank you KEVIN OLSEN at W. W. NORTON for always being there.

My parents and siblings are my biggest fans, and I appreciate their encouragement (and their ability to keep me humble along the way): CHARLES and YVONNE PALMISANO, ROSANNE PALMISANO and SEAN ROY, JULIE and CURT ANDERSON, CHARLIE and BRENDA PALMISANO.

Thank you to my best friend, SHANNON QUIMBY, who is just as passionate about salvage as I am, and other dear friends and family who have this passion as well, and who support me wholeheartedly: KIM and CLIFF DEETJEN, TRUEXCULLINS ARCHITECTURE and INTERIOR DESIGN, PEREGRINE DESIGN/BUILD, TAWNYA PELL, KARIN LIDBECK-BRENT, TINA NOEL, HEATHER and ANDREW LYNDS, MAD RIVER BARN, JEN WYMAN, BRIAN GOODYEAR, BOB BEACH, PENNIE BEACH, and the entire BASIN HARBOR family.

And to old and new friends and acquaintances, thank you. What a wonderful trip this has been. Thank you to: PAIGE MANNING, CAROL and RANDY DUPREE, DAVID KNOX, BRIAN BARCLAY, MASON BROTHERS ARCHITECTURAL SALVAGE, DAVID BOOTH, PAMELA PETERS, FIVE CORNER ANTIQUES, CONANT METAL & LIGHT, NATHAN GOOD, NATHAN GOOD ARCHITECTS, BEDROCK INDUSTRIES, JUNK GYPSY COMPANY, AMIE SIKES, JOLIE SIKES, AMY "ARCHIE" ALLEN, KELLEY KEEN, PAIGE and SMOOT HULL, THE VINTAGE ROUND TOP, WENDY LEWIS, THE TEXTILE TRUNK, RENEE TORNABENE, BULB to BLOSSOM, JENNIFER and FRED MYERS, JENNIFER'S GARDEN AUSTIN, RYAN SULLIVAN, ALBINO NICASIO, LUIS VASQUEZ, RACHEL and PRESTON BROWNING, SALVAGE WORKS, LELAND DUCK, CHELSEA HOWARD, REVIVE UPHOLSTERY & DESIGN, TRICIA ROSE, JANE COSLICK, JANE COSLICK'S DESIGNS and RESTORATIONS, EMILY and CALVIN SELLERS, UMLAND STREET SUNDAY HAUS, BARRY and SUSIE FANTICH, DAVE JONAH, SHELBURNE FARMS, GEORGE and RACHAEL RAMOS, GEORGE RAMOS WOODWORKING, BILL RAYMER, DONNA LEE ROBERTSON, RESTORATION RESOURCES, PRINCE COFFEE, CHELSEA and BRANDT KAEMINGK, MAKE KING DESIGN, LIZZY, LUIS, and PIPPA, BRETT BUNDOCK, GIDEON POLLACK, ADAM HILL, FIRECLAY TILE, CARI CUCKSEY, VINCENT LAFANO, EDNA and MARK STEPHENS, REPURPOSE PAINT, JACKIE MCGILVERY, DIY NETWORK, KIM CLEMENTS and JOE SCHNEIDER, JAS DESIGN BUILD, TERRY HANCOCK, RESOURCE BUILDING MATERIAL STORE, KATHY

LEAVESLEY, FIFTH THIRD BANK WOMEN'S SERIES, TINA LANGELOH, HOME and SALVAGE, KIM RAWLINS, STEPHANIE WILLIAMS, SWEET SALVAGE, JESSE WHITE, SARASOTA ARCHITECTURAL SALVAGE, JEREMY and ADELE SMITH, BARGE CANAL MARKETPLACE, ALL the FOLKS at the COUNTRY LIVING FAIRS, BETTY LYN WALTERS-ELLER, PEGGY VALENTINO, and all the amazing people from STELLA SHOWS who make me feel like family. Thank you to MICHELLE DE LA VEGA, PATTI MORENO and ROBERT PATTON-SPRUILL, PATRICK, KAREN, and BONNIE KENNY, SOUTH PORCH ANTIQUES, BILL DREW, HMC ADVERTISING, TOM CROSS, CHAMPLAIN VALLEY ANTIQUES, MICHAEL BODGE, MICHELLE CHEUNG, FLOR CARPET TILES, LUCINDA HUTSON, BEVERLY MARTINETS, BEL SOLÉ BED & BREAKFAST, VINTAGE BAZAAR, JESSICA HELGERSON, JESSICA HELGERSON INTERIOR DESIGN, KELLY GEISEN, KELLY GEISEN DESIGNS, GARDENER'S SUPPLY COMPANY, GOODWILL INDUSTRIES, HABITAT for HUMANITY, SIMPLY SPRAY, MARY HEINRICH ALOI, VINTAGE INSPIRED MARKETPLACE, JUNE and WENDELL ANDERSON, THE BUNDY MODERN, CARA WALKER, MARK and KIM GAYNOR, LIVING VINTAGE, LORI JENSEN, and a big huge group hug to all the homeowners who remained anonymous and all the builders, designers, and professionals who worked on these salvaged homes.

Without my husband and daughter, STEPHEN and GABRIELLE, this book would not be in your hands. They have encouraged and supported my passion for working with salvage for as long as we can all remember. I'm a lucky lady.

Credits

Interior Design/DIY Credits

ALL INTERIOR DESIGNS AND DIY PROJECTS BY JOANNE PALMISANO, UNLESS NOTED BELOW.

COVER: Joanne Palmisano, homeowners Andrew and Heather Lynds

P. 2   Chelsea & Brandt Kaemingk, Make King Design

P. 6   Joanne Palmisano, homeowner Gideon Pollack

P. 8   Shannon Quimby

P. 11   Emily and Calvin Sellers

P. 12   Tricia Rose

P. 14   Jane Coslick Designs and Restorations

P. 18   Wendy Lewis

P. 21   Jennifer and Fred Myers, Jennifer's Gardens & Guest House

P. 22   Rachel and Preston Browning, Salvage Works

P. 25   Joanne and Rosanne Palmisano

P. 30   Leland Duck, Revive Upholstery and Design

P. 33   Joanne Palmisano; tile by Fireclay

P. 36   Restoration Resources, Boston; DIY by Joanne Palmisano

P. 40   Kim Deetjen, Truexcullins Architecture and Interior Design, and Cliff Deetjen, Peregrine Design/Build

P. 42   (right) Carol and Randy Dupree

P. 45   (bottom) Carol and Randy Dupree

P. 47   Leland Duck and Chelsea Howard, Revive Upholstery and Design

P. 48   Chelsea & Brandt Kaemingk of Make King Design

P. 49   Terry Hancock and Nathan Good Architects

P. 51   (left) George and Rachel Ramos, George Ramos Cabinetry

P. 51   (right) Shannon Quimby

P. 53   Emily and Calvin Sellers

P. 54   (top) Prince Coffee Shop and Revive Shared Studio Space

P. 54   (bottom) Chelsea & Brandt Kaemingk of Make King Design

P. 57   Tricia Rose

P. 58   Joanne Palmisano, Heather and Andrew Lynds

P. 62   Joanne Palmisano and Stephen Booth

P. 63   Jeremy and Adele Smith, Barge Canal Market

P. 68   Joanne Palmisano, homeowner Gideon Pollack

P. 74   Carol and Randy Dupree

P. 76   Karen and Patrick Kenny, South Porch Antiques

P. 84   Barge Canal Market

P. 85   Salvage Works, Portland, Oregon

P. 86   Joanne Palmisano, homeowners, Andrew and Heather Lynds

P. 88   Chelsea & Brandt Kaemingk, Make King Design, Portland, Homeowners, Michael Bodge and Michelle Cheung

P. 91   Salvage Works, Tim Brock

P. 92   Jennifer and Fred Myers

P. 94   Kim Deetjen, Truexcullins Architecture and Interior Design, and Cliff Deetjen, Peregrine Design/Build

P. 97   Jennifer and Fred Myers

P. 98   Architectural design by Jim Edgcomb, interior by Joanne Palmisano

P.100   Lucinda Hutson

P.101   Joanne Palmisano, homeowners June and Wendell Anderson

P.102   Emily and Calvin Sellers

P. 110   Revive Upholstery and Design Textiles, Joanne Palmisano

P. 112   Champlain Valley Antiques Center

P. 113   Kim Deetjen, Truexcullins Architecture and Interior Design, and Cliff Deetjen, Peregrine Design/Build

P. 114   (right) Shannon Quimby

P. 114   (left) Emily and Calvin Sellers

P. 115   Kim Clements and Joe Schneider, J.A.S. Design Build

P. 116   Paige Manning

P. 117   (left) Paige Manning

P. 118   Beverly Martinets and Joanne Palmisano

P. 119   Joanne Palmisano, Bev Martinet, and Susan Teare

P. 120   Jennifer's Gardens Guest House

Photo Credits

ALL PHOTOGRAPHS BY SUSAN TEARE, UNLESS NOTED BELOW.

PHOTOS BY JOANNE PALMISANO:

PP.24, 25 (bottom right), 33 (bottom right), 37 (bottom right), 39 (bottom right), 56, 66 (bottom right), 68, (bottom left), 71 (bottom right), 96, 99 (bottom left),105, 107 (bottom right), 112, 119, 125 (bottom right), 127, 130, 131 (bottom right), 132 (bottom left), 134, (bottom left), 137 (bottom right), 141 (before picture), 144 (upper right), 145 (bottom right), 153 (bottom right), 155 (bottom right), 173 (bottom right), 177 (bottom right), 179 (bottom right), 181, 183, 185, 197 (bottom right), 207, 208 (bottom right), 211 (bottom right)

P.42   (left) photo courtesy of Lindsay Raymond-
          jack Photography
P. 65   www.GarySweetman.com
P.121   April Pizana
P.149   Gaynor Photography
P.150   photo by Jeff Clarke
P.159   Gaynor Photography
P.170   photo by Jeff Clarke

Index

NOTE: *Italicized* pages refer to photos.